In the beginning, GOD created...

In the beginning, GOD created...
A consideration of Biblical Creation

J. H. John Peet

Grace Publications

GRACE PUBLICATIONS TRUST
139 Grosvenor Avenue
London N5 2NH
England

Managing Editors
J. P. Arthur, M.A.
H.J. Appleby

ISBN 0 946462 31 3

Distributed by Evangelical Press, 12 Wooler Street, Darlington,
Co Durham, DL1 1RQ.

Art work — Anne Lock BVSC, MRCVS and Jonathan Rayfield
(Aspect Graphics).

Cover design 'The earth was formless and empty' (Gen 1:2).

Printed in Great Britain by the Bath Press, Avon

Contents

List of illustrations

'... the origin of the cosmos and the causal principles of its history remain unexplained and inaccessible to science. Here is hidden the First Cause sought by theology and philosophy. The First Cause is not known and I suspect that it will never be known to living man. We may, if we are so inclined, worship it in our own ways, but we certainly do not comprehend it'. G G Simpson ('The Meaning of Evolution', Yale University Press, New Haven, 1967).

'Can a man by searching find out God'? Job 11:7

'This is what we speak, not in words taught us by human wisdom but in words taught by the Spirit.' 1 Corinthians 2:13

Introduction

Many books have been written on the theme of origins, not least in contrasting Creation and evolution. Any new book on the subject should be sufficiently different in its approach or content to justify its production.

This little book is written to examine the biblical record on origins and to examine confirmatory evidence that can be observed around us. It is not attempting to contrast evolution and Creation directly. Consequently, it does not claim to examine every relevant issue nor to consider each issue in depth. It is assumed that the reader starts from a similar theological base to the author, that is, that the Bible is the Word of God and our primary source of God's revelation, utterly reliable in all that it affirms.

Some years ago, Professor E J Young wrote a study on Genesis chapter one ('Studies in Genesis One'; Presbyterian and Reformed Publishing Co., Philadelphia, 1964). It is still relevant today. He says, 'The first verse of Genesis ... stands as a simple declaration of the fact of absolute creation' (p. 7). The writer is stating that the heaven and earth had a beginning and this beginning is to be found in the fact that God created them. Again, he states (p. 43), that, as the Word of God, 'whenever it speaks on any subject, whatever that subject may be, [the Bible] is accurate in what it says.' So, regarding Genesis 1, 'Our principal task ... is to get at the meaning which the writer sought to convey'. We have no other objective in this book.

We read that by God's word the world was created — so it was designed. Again, we read that by God's word, the world was judged — so it was deluged. These are unambiguous statements.

There are some topics which are conjectural and still the subject of scientific research. If this publication reaches a second edition, some of the interpretations of the natural record may have to be revised in the light of research! So the reader should trust the biblical record and take the applications as tentative.

An appendix is included to give an introduction to the structure of the cell for those unacquainted with it. There is also an appendix discussing the limitations of radiometric dating methods. Biblical quotations are normally from the New International Version (published by Hodder and Stoughton).

The author acknowledges the invaluable help of colleagues of the Biblical Creation Society and contributors to their journal 'Origins'. In particular, I would express thanks to David Tyler, Michael Garton, Paul Garner and Joachim Scheven for their work on geology from which I have drawn. My thanks are due to Kevin Charman for the development of some of the diagrams (especially figures 6 and 12). The final art work has been produced for me by Anne Lock and by Aspect Graphics, Harrogate.

Thanks are also due to my father, James H Peet, who through my childhood, pointed me in the right direction. Finally, I dedicate this work to my wife, Ruth, who has supported me in it and sat through untold lectures!

Above all, to God be the glory.

J H John Peet

1.
'In the beginning, God created...'

Several years ago, Professor Sidney Fox (a leading evolutionist) published an article[1] entitled 'In the beginning, life assembled itself ..'. This was a clear challenge to the biblical statement (Genesis 1:1) and declared the contrast: God or no-God was responsible for the origin of life. The battle-ground is clear. Some try to fuse the two approaches producing 'theistic evolution' or 'creation by evolution'. Such attempts are made by honest people and often clever people, but there is, we believe, a great gulf between the two views which cannot be bridged.[2]

As will be seen, biblical theology develops from the Creation account and so any watering down of the biblical record has a wider theological implication. Orthodox biblical theology has been clearly developed from the unfolding revelation starting with the Creation account. There is a challenge here to the 'theistic evolutionist' to produce a consistent theology from his position.

If Genesis 1 — 11 is not factual history, what is meant by Adam as the 'son of God'? What happens to biblical genealogies? What about the biblical teaching on woman? How do we account for the origin of evil, suffering and death? Arising from this, what is meant by Christ as the 'last Adam'? What is the purpose of Christ's death — and so his resurrection? What is meant by the concept of redemption? But, more on these questions later.

If a case is tried in court, the legal counsel attempts to prove its case by calling witnesses and presenting material evidence. When considering origins, most protagonists believe there cannot be any witnesses (because it pre-dates life, by definition) and also that the scientific evidences are unambiguously supportive of evolution. But this is not the case.

There was a witness! God himself. The three Persons of the Godhead were there and have testified. The Bible is their testimony and any honest assessment of the case must consider their statement. It is not our purpose in this book to consider the reliability and understanding of Scripture. That is adequately covered elsewhere.[3]

Nature of science

Science is variously defined. Some assume, for example, that evolution is science. In fact, evolution is only a theory or model by which some scientists attempt to explain origins. Rather, it is a term used to describe a variety of theories which seek to explain the origin of life by no-God. Some of these approaches are incompatible, but they have a common objective: a mechanistic explanation of the physical universe.

In the media, science is often elevated to a level which is inconsistent with its nature. For example, one hears comments like, 'Science says ...' or 'Science has shown ...' At best, what is meant is that 'Some scientists say ...' or 'A scientist has demonstrated ...'

The term 'science' can be used to describe the identification of observable facts and the attempts to explain them. It is the study of natural phenomena and the search for an explanation within the natural laws. A scientist seeks a suitable cause to explain an observed fact or set of facts. Obviously this implies that an explanation is possible. One might question whether this is a logical position for those who take the no-God stance. Why should there be an explanation? Who established the natural laws?

Modern science, with its belief in logical explanations, was developed by scientists who were themselves Christians. Because they believed God worked to a purpose, they also believed they should be able to identify order in his world.

The scientist will seek to test his explanations according to rules that the scientific community have developed. Generally, attempts are made to explain processes mechanistically — that is, without human intervention. This is one difference between the sciences and the social sciences. For example, the scientist writes in an impersonal and passive mood, whereas a sociologist writes in a personal and active sense. The scientist tries to avoid interfering in a process and explains it that way. This is alright, provided neither he nor anyone else has intervened in some way.

For example, a scientist seeing a ball falling in front of a cliff face will be interested in the laws of motion and not the young lad who has just hit his ball 'for a six' and lost it. BUT, his explanation is inadequate because it is incomplete.

However, this can also be an incorrect explanation. A forensic scientist finds materials from the scene of a crime and proposes (based on evidence and his experience) the process behind their occurrence there. BUT, in court, the defence might bring in testimony to show that his reconstruction, though feasible, is false.

The American National Academy of Sciences defined the most basic characteristic of science as a *reliance upon naturalistic explanations*. This was deliberately formulated to exclude from scientific consideration anything that involved God. An explanation of origins based on no-God does not prove that there was no-God involved. Indeed, the creationist will argue that there is evidence of God's involvement.

So, we will use the observable evidence around us, believing that, if God's record is true, it will conform to his written testimony.

Reasoning and logic are good gifts of God, but they are not sufficient of themselves. 'Can a man by searching find out God?' (Job 11:7). Can logic discover, or explain, salvation? An interesting illustration of this truth is found in 2 Kings 6:8-14. The king of Aram (Syria) was fighting Israel. In his war council, he planned to trap the Israelites at one place after another, but, on each occasion, they avoided his ambush. The meetings had taken place in an inner chamber and could not be overheard. There was one logical explanation — there was an Israelite spy in his council. But, the truth was different: it was revealed to the prophet Elisha by God and he told the king of Israel. This was not a solution to be deduced by human intellect. The same is true of the investigation of the origins of life.

We recognize — and do not apologize for it — that our position is based on faith. Hebrews 11:3 says, 'By faith we understand that the universe was formed at God's command, so that what is seen was not made out of what was visible'. It is significant that the conclusions were not those that are ultimately testable (e.g. that the world is spherical), for such conclusions would make the Bible out of date. The basic conclusion of faith is something that is not testable. We do not measure our belief in Creation by what we now know : that would be limiting the power of God. Our faith transcends the provable. The basis of our faith is also clear from that passage: it is faith in God. He is unimpeachable. His Word is thoroughly reliable.

We are working, therefore, from the Bible as our source. If we exclude the Bible as the primary source of revelation, then our case is pointless.

Creation record is historical

It is often argued that the Genesis account is mythical. The New Testament writers did not think so. Whenever they referred to it, they clearly regarded it as a piece of historical narrative. Consider, for example, these aspects of the Creation account and the New Testament references:

It is by the Word of God	Hebrews 11:3
The emerging earth	2 Peter 3:5
God's first decree	2 Corinthians 4:6
The creation of herbs	Hebrews 6:7
Filling of the earth with inhabitants	Acts 17:24
Man made in God's image	1 Corinthians 11:7
Creation of man	Mark 19:4; 10:6

A number of words are used in the Bible to describe the origin of the world and, in particular, man. This is demonstrated in Isaiah 43:7, 'Even everyone that is called by my name; for I have *created* him for my glory, I have *formed* him; yea, I have *made* him.' The same three words are used in the Creation account: 'God said, Let us *make* man in our image ... So God *created* man in his own image ... And the LORD God *formed* man of the dust of the ground.' (Genesis 1:26,27; 2:7). They are used also of the earth in Isaiah 45:18. The words cr*eate* and *formed* are applied in Isaiah uniquely to the works of God. The three words are similar in meaning but have a slightly different emphasis. All three are necessary to describe adequately the work of God.

It is not our intention to evaluate the evolutionary theory directly. The reader will draw his or her own conclusions on this matter. However, it ought to be realised that it is not surprising if evolutionists can point to supporting evidence for their position. No theory, good or bad, will be produced in isolation from the evidence.

Even a lawyer for a guilty person can usually find some evidence which suggests that his client is innocent! The evidence may conform to the rules of the evolutionist's paradigm, but are the rules correct?

We will consider the biblical testimony and look at the world around us to see if they are in agreement and how we are to understand this world in the light of the biblical revelation.

What was God's purpose in creation? God's plan was to make someone like himself. This person he called 'man'. He provided him with a place to live, in which to work and over which to rule. So, he made the world. It is important to recognize that the rest of creation was secondary to this purpose. This is declared directly and indirectly in various places and contexts. The sabbath rest was instituted for man's sake (Mark 2:27). Nature is cursed for man's sake, as a punishment to remind man that he is dependent on God alone (Genesis 3:17; Romans 8:20-23). And, as the catechism says, 'Man's chief end is to glorify God and to enjoy him for ever'.

References
1. S Fox, New Scientist, 1969, 450.
2. D Tyler, 'Theistic Evolution', Biblical Creation Society discussion paper.
3. For example:
   W Kuhrt, 'Interpreting the Bible,' Grace Publications (1990)
   C C Pond, 'The Authority of Scripture', Origins, 1992, 5(13), 3-9.

2.
Created on purpose and for a purpose.

The opening words of the Scriptures state that 'In the beginning, *God* created the heavens and the earth'. In fact, the whole of Genesis 1 is very clear and specific — by him all things were made and without him there was nothing made (John 1:3). On each of the days of creation, we read that 'God said' and then we are told that it was done. It was not a matter of God setting things in motion and then sitting back to observe it and see what happened. He acted deliberately at each stage.

At the end of the six days of activity, he rested from the work that he had done. This was not a rest due to tiredness, but a rest (a cessation) due to a work completed. It had been finished. This is what the record says: 'Thus the heavens and the earth were completed in all their vast array. By the seventh day God had finished the work he had been doing; so on the seventh day he rested from all his work' (Genesis 2:2).

His method of creation was of two kinds. Sometimes he created material from nothing (Hebrews 11:3; Romans 4:17). On other occasions, he used previously created material as a basis for a new creation. The former is described as 'absolute creation' and the latter as 'mediate creation'. In both cases, his action was purposeful and deliberate and so is described as 'Special Creation'.

We are told that God created by speaking. At his command, the earth and its living order came into being. (See also Psalms 33:9 and 148:5). Jesus Christ is the Word of God. So, John tells us that it was by him that the worlds were created. (See also Colossians 1:16). We are also told that God's Spirit moved across the face of the waters

(Genesis 1:2; Psalm 104:30). His Spirit also made man a living soul (Genesis 2:7). So, the whole Trinity was active in the creation — its planning and execution.

The mode of creation is stated quite specifically: it is *by his word* (Proverbs 33:6,8,9; 2 Peter 2:5) and *by his wisdom* (Proverbs 8:22-31; Psalm 104:24). This is in clear contrast to any naturalistic explanation.

We note too that the rest of Scripture makes it plain that God is the Creator:

1 Chronicles 16:26	- of the heavens
Psalm 95:5	- of the sea and land
Isaiah 44:24	- of all things
Isaiah 45:18	- of the heavens and the earth and their inhabitants
Acts 17:24-25	- of the heavens and earth
Acts 14:15	- of the heaven, earth, sea and everything in them
Colossians 1:15-17	- of all things
Hebrews 1:2-3	- of the universe

This tells us that creation was a deliberate act. (See Romans 9:19-22). It was not chance. It was not a game or pastime which could be rejected if it did not work. The act was deliberate in its conception and completion. Since it was the work of an all-wise God, we would expect it to be perfect in its design work. The believer in 'creation by design' expects to find plenty of evidence of design in nature.

Before turning to some examples, it is necessary to emphasize that there are many of them and some are too complex to cover here and the reader is advised to look elsewhere.

Bombardier beetle

Consider, in the first place, the bombardier beetle (*Brachinus*). Though believers in 'creation by design' have long drawn attention to this amazing creature, only recently have the believers in the no-God process started to admit their bewilderment. We will consider only the defence mechanism to illustrate our point, but the whole creature is the result of design. When under attack, this beetle emits hot, toxic gases.

These gases are generated by a reaction between two chemicals, hydrogen peroxide and hydroquinone. So, firstly, we have the design of a metabolism to generate these two compounds in sufficient quantity to be effective. The Designer had to know that it was these two chemicals that were required. Other chemicals would not have been so suitable. But, there is a problem: they react slowly to produce their products (steam, oxygen and quinone), too slowly to be a defence mechanism. Another substance, a catalyst, is required. A catalyst accelerates the reaction to an instantaneous process. Thus, a suitable catalyst has to be designed and stored separately, only being injected at the right moment! Catalysts are very specific and they are very complex in their chemical composition and imply specific design rather than chance origin.

However, to store the chemicals indefinitely would be a problem. The reaction may be slow, but it does occur and would cause the beetle to explode, or eject the products prematurely. To overcome this, the Divine Chemist provided an 'inhibitor'. This is another specific chemical which, in this case, prevents reaction until the catalyst is added. So, four metabolic processes have to be designed to generate these materials, not to mention the appropriate organs to store them and initiate the reaction. It speaks clearly of design and so a Designer.

Woodpecker

Another example of design is the woodpecker. Again, we will concentrate on specific functions rather than the complete creature. This bird feeds on insects found deep in a tree. It hammers at the trunk with its beak until it has drilled a hole. Of course, we could consider the essential design of the beak, but think instead of what such hammering would do to the bird's head. It hammers at up to ten times a second for six hours. We would not recommend any other creature to try it! It would shatter the skull. In the woodpecker, there is a 'shock absorber' between the beak and the cranium. This is extremely efficient. In addition, as the beak hits the tree, a muscle pulls the cranium back. To enable it to maintain its balance during this process, each foot has two forward claws (in contrast to the common 3-to-1 pattern in birds). In addition, the stiff, elastic tail

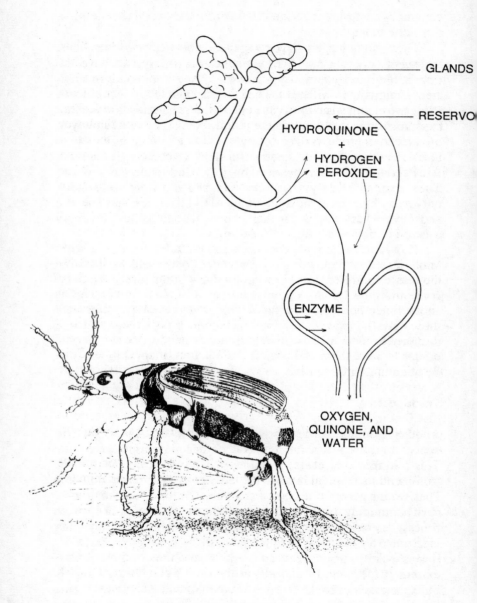

GLANDS

RESERVO[IR]

HYDROQUINONE
+
HYDROGEN
PEROXIDE

ENZYME

OXYGEN,
QUINONE, AND
WATER

Figure 1: The Bombardier Beetle.

feathers bend and spread against the trunk forming an effective support. Precise engineering!

But, it would not be sufficient to drill a hole unless the bird were able to reach the insects. To do this, it has a tongue which is five times as long as that normally possessed by a bird. Where can it store such a long tongue without the risk of choking itself — or at least filling the mouth so no food can get into it? Another unique design. The hyoid bone that controls the tongue passes through the lower jaw up behind and over the cranium and is anchored in the front nostril! The tongue is like a spearhead with a number of backward pointing barbs. It is also coated with a sticky substance. These enable it to catch the insects. Such clever design work may make us marvel, but it is to be expected of our God.

Humming bird

Another fascinating bird is the humming bird. This tiny bird has about three hundred different variations (covering wide variations in colour, in beak shape and length, and size) but there are unique facets which speak of specific design. It has a hovering system allowing it to move forward or backwards. To do this, it adopts a body angle of 45°, achieving a horizontal wing beat. The wings beat at 50 — 80 times a second and the bird flies at 90 km per hour. Only the humming bird has rigid wings, which are necessary to generate power on each stroke of the cycle. The energy consumption is huge and has been estimated as being equivalent to a human being eating 13000 hamburgers a day! The consumption of so much food to produce that much energy requires a sophisticated metabolic system.

Alongside this, it has a heart beat rate of 1260 per minute (compared to a typical human heart rate of around 70 per minute). That would generate a body temperature of 385°C — an oven-roasted humming bird! So, it drinks the equivalent of sixty litres of water a day to keep cool. The bill is long and narrow so that it can reach into a flower to extract the nectar, without damaging the plant. (In one variety of the humming bird, the beak is curved and fits uniquely to one plant — and only this bird can pollinate that flower). The tongue has a curved 'w' shape to enable it to hold the nectar and, like the woodpecker, can be extracted into the back of its head.

Figure 2: Humming Bird and Woodpecker.

Bird flight

The most obvious feature of a bird is its flight, yet even this speaks of design. In order to fly, the bird must generate a lot of energy (as mentioned above for the humming bird). The breast muscles have to be very powerful and are up to 30% of the body weight (only 1% in man!). The concentration of sugar in the blood is twice that in the animal world. As a consequence of this high body temperature, a rapid circulation and an efficient digestive system, the birds utilize a relatively high proportion of their diet.

This efficiency is demonstrated by a migrating bird. For example, the golden plover migrates thousands of miles from Canada to mid-southern America. In that journey, it loses only 57g of body weight. A light aircraft working to a similar level of efficiency would get 60 km per litre rather than 7 km per litre.

The oxygen required to 'burn up' the food is delivered by the lungs, but these have a totally different structure from the lungs of other vertebrates, even though they are virtually identical in all birds. Since the rate of consumption of the food is high, the rate of oxygen supply must also be fast. The conventional animal heart is too slow and a one-way system was provided for the birds. The result is the flow of a greater volume per second. Recently (1992) some workers have located the valve which controls the flow direction and rate. Muscles in the wall of the first part of the lung act as a variable constriction. When the bird is at rest, the valve is constricted, but it is relaxed when the bird is in flight.

To capture their food, the birds of prey have an eyesight with a resolution ten times that of man, enabling it to detect its prey at a vast distance. It is reported that pigeons are being trained to detect people in distress in the sea, for example, and so communicate their location to the rescue services.

The important functioning part of the bird in its flight is the wing. The feathers are also able to protect the bird against the extremes of heat and cold, but let us concentrate on the flight characteristics. The feathers have an intricate design. The shaft is hollow, making it light, but it is strong. It is stronger than any man-made material. The shaft has branches, called barbs, which are arranged diagonally along the shaft. Smaller branches on this are known as *barbules*. These overlap with neighbouring barbules, linking together by means of hooks.

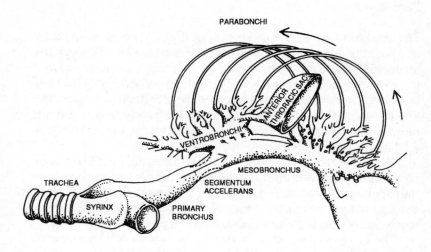

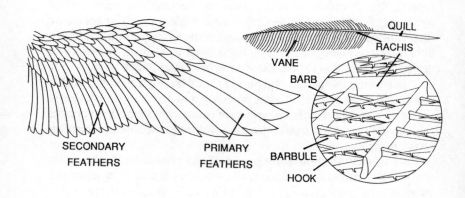

Figure 3: Structure of a bird's lung and feather.

In flight, about one million barbules cooperate in this way to give an air-resistant surface. There are tendons which allow the feathers to twist and open in order to reduce wind resistance on the upward movement of the wing. The structure functions in a similar manner to a zip-fastner.

Near the quill, there are nerve endings embedded in the skin. These are sensitive to the precise position of each feather. Through the central nervous system, this information is transmitted to the brain causing adjustment to over twelve thousand muscles controlling the feathers. Precision engineering by a brilliant Designer or a random coincidence by a no-God process? And, in the latter case, what did the feather (indeed the whole bird) develop from? There is no feasible precursor to these structures. Of course, the feathers are only one aspect of a fully integrated flight system which affects the skeleton, nervous, muscular and metabolic systems.

The giraffe

The giraffe and its long neck has always been a source of speculation. But, it is not just a matter of a long neck (or how it got it). Because the brain is at such a height (up to three metres above the heart), an extra large heart (0.6 metre long and 12 kg in weight) is necessary to supply an adequate blood supply. The blood pressure is, therefore, high (three times that in man). But, what happens when it bends its head to ground level to eat or drink (perhaps two metres below the heart)? This would cause the blood to rush to the head and result in serious brain damage. To avoid this, three design features are needed. It spreads its front legs apart to lower the heart level. Then the jugular veins have one-way valves which prevent the blood rushing to the head when it is lowered or flowing from the head when it is raised. The third feature is a mass of spongy tissue at the base of the brain. This soaks up any excess blood flowing from the carotid artery. All these features are required to achieve a working design for the creature.

The blood

Let's stay with the blood for a moment. The human blood system (as with an animal's) contains a substance essential to its ability to transport oxygen, a gas necessary for respiration. This substance is

Figure 4: The giraffe.

called *haemoglobin*. The molecule is complex in structure, consisting, essentially, of an iron atom in a protein cage. Normally, iron in an oxygen environment is converted to rust. The process is not reversible; the iron loses its chemical activity and physical properties. In blood, the iron takes up the oxygen at the lungs and releases it wherever necessary around the body. To achieve this result, a special structure is essential and is found in the haemoglobin. A study of the molecule shows that there is a hydrophobic (i.e. water-repelling) 'pocket' in the protein, surrounding the iron, which prevents the conversion of the iron to rust.

Furthermore, the overall structure of the haemoglobin (and so the pocket just mentioned) is determined by the protein structure. A strand of the protein chain contains about 300 basic units called *amino acids*. An error in one unit can have serious consequences. For example, the seventh unit should be glutamic acid. But, if valine is substituted in error, the resulting haemoglobin is much less efficient, giving rise to the fatal sickle cell anaemia. This error, in turn, results from just one fault in 900 hundred units in the gene for the formation of this protein.

The haemoglobin is packed into a cell of unique but critical shape (see the figure). The cell has to have the maximum possible surface area (so that it can absorb the maximum amount of oxygen) and yet enable the gas to migrate rapidly to the haemoglobin packing it. The shape of the blood cell is the optimum to achieve these two goals simultaneously. The cell also has to be very flexible so that it can move through the large arteries and the narrow capillaries as well. It must also be able to revert back to its original shape on release from the constriction. Again, the actual shape of the molecule is ideal for this. The sickle cell results in a different and less efficient shape. The cell also has to be strong, being subject to great pressure and a lot of flexing during its lifetime of 120 days. The body's regenerative mechanism is synchronized with this lifetime. Again, the sickle cell is more fragile, so has a much shorter lifetime. The time difference is the cause of the anaemia.

T4 bacteriophage

Often it is assumed that the smallest organisms are the simplest (a result of the assumption that all living things developed from simpler ones and became increasingly complex). One of the small-

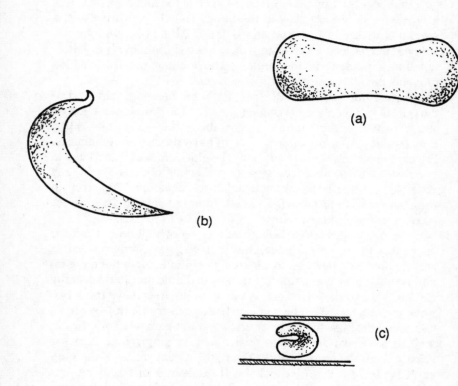

Figure 5: The red blood cell.
a. Normal   b. Sickle   c. Normal cell passing through a capillary.

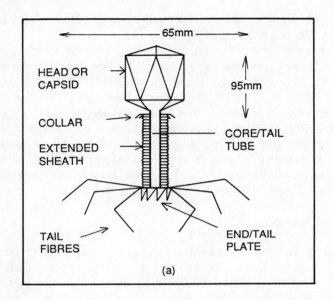

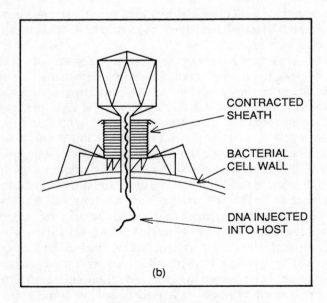

Figure 6: T4 bacteriophage

est things is a bacteriophage. This is a virus that infects bacteria! Consider the T4 bacteriophage.

It is essentially an automatic hypodermic syringe which is less than 1/5000th of a millimetre long. This virus has to identify the host bacterium, attach itself to it and then inject DNA, the genetic material in living matter. Having been injected, the DNA is then able to reproduce itself in the host. But look at the design of the syringe. It has to be able to attach its tail fibres to the cell wall so that the tail plate is correctly positioned for the injection. It has to have a tail sheath that is able to contract and thereby insert the needle, the tail tube, through which the DNA will pass. Quite a feat of engineering by a no-God process lacking intelligence or direction!

Vestigial organs

Another implication of God's design in creation is that there are no vestigial organs. Those who imagine origin by a no-God process have to postulate the loss of use of certain organs, followed by their eventual replacement. These are described as *vestigial*. Typical examples have included the human coccyx and appendix. From a list that extended to over one hundred such items, we now know of none! Research has shown that these organs do have a function, just as predicted by divine creation.

The human appendix, for example, is now known to be a vital source of defence against infection. The appendix is a small append-age at the end of the caecum. This part of the intestine is particularly important in animals that live on vegetation (for example, grass) rather than on meat. It generates the enzymes needed for the digestion of cellulose in the plants. In mankind, this is only a small organ and is assumed by many to be a remnant of our animal ancestry. (This is evidence of design to meet the requirement of the human diet!) So, the caecum and the appendix are assumed to be without function. In the past, the appendix was removed at any sign of trouble. Research has demonstrated what the believer in design has always known: it does have a function. In sickness, a person may suffer from diarrhoea which wipes the bowels clean of the protective substances. The appendix is a specialised structure which acts as a reservoir of antibody-producing cells which provide a protective system in such circumstances. It is believed by some research workers that there may be a higher incidence of bowel disease in people that have had an appendectomy than amongst those who have retained the appendix.

The coccyx is a triangular group of bones situated at the base of the spinal column. Those who believe in the development of human beings from the primates (the ape family) claim that this is the residual tail of such creatures. But is this a true analysis of the coccyx?

These bones are very different in their structure from those of the vertebral column and so of a tail. Instead, they have grooves to which are attached ligaments and muscles. These muscles form the floor of the pelvis and are the principal part of the diaphragm and supply a support for the rectum. In females, these muscles are also important in aiding the process of childbirth. Rather than being a useless vestige of a former animal form, the coccyx is an essential part of the human anatomy, speaking of design, not accident.

God's fingerprints

In life, if we are confronted with the work of an artist, we expect it to involve the characteristics we associate with him or her. Each artist has his or her own style. This is found in pictures, sculptures and literature, for example. There is no reason why we should not expect God to leave his 'fingerprints' too.

In the nucleus of the cell, we find a material called DNA (deoxyribonucleic acid). This is the cell's 'instruction manual'. It directs the production of materials and functions of the cell. It consists of a chemical code in which each cluster of three chemical groups (called 'bases') relates to one amino acid to be used in the chemical synthesis. If there were a common Designer behind living systems, we could reasonably expect that this code would occur right across the living world. And it does. Though God has given us a world of variety, there is no need to produce more than one perfect design code, though it might be appropriate to have small differences between different systems.

A beautiful painting (or, indeed, an ugly one) will tell us something about the character of the artist. This is true of the world in which we live. Even though it has been spoilt by sin (see chapter 6), it still says a lot about its Creator. The table summarizes this. It all speaks of his beauty and love of it.

(a) The earth speaks of God's ...

goodness	Psalm 147:9; Acts 14:17
authority	Proverbs 8:27-29
eternity	Psalm 90:1-2
immutability	Psalm 102:25-27
omnipresence	Jeremiah 23:24
transcendency	Psalm 97:9
keeping power	Psalm 121:2; Romans 1:20

(b) The heavens declare God's ...

glory	Psalm 19:1
immensity	Isaiah 48:13
power	Psalm 33:6; Jeremiah 32:17
faithfulness	Psalm 36:5
mercy	Genesis 9:13
wisdom	Psalm 136:5
righteousness	Psalm 97:6

To deny his creative work is to rob oneself of the consequent assurance. If he did not make the heavens and the earth, where is our confidence in his keeping power to come from (Psalm 121:2)? If he did not make the heavens by the word of his power (Psalm 33:6), why should the earth stand in awe of him (Psalm 33:7-8)?

Creation is a material display of God's invisible qualities, his divine nature (Romans 1:20). As we look into it with the eyes of faith (Hebrews 11:3), we will see something of his nature. A valuable lesson is to be learnt from Job. As he and his friends questioned God's actions towards him, God responded with a series of questions (Job chapters 38-41). The questions are based on nature. Can you answer these questions, Job? So, what right have you to question God's actions? Job's reaction is short and to the point: 'I am unworthy. How can I reply to you? I cover my mouth with my hand ... I will say no more'. (40:4). The questions are still relevant today. They leave us without excuse (Romans 1:20); God has clearly displayed his power and authority, to which we must bow.

Isaiah (45:18) indicates that the Lord created the world for a purpose and that was its inhabitation. (A no-God process has no purpose). Comparison with Isaiah 44:26-28 makes it clear that it is humanity that is the intended inhabitant.

3.
The time factor

The Bible opens by declaring that *'In the beginning* God created the heavens and the earth'. Time had begun. This is a profound statement scientifically. The philosophers have been trying to grapple with the subject of time. Many, even believers in creation, have found much to argue about when relating time to biblical history, but let's consider some of the biblical facts.

Firstly, these early chapters of Genesis are written in an historical form consistent with the rest of the book. A lot of people try to dismiss or diminish the truth of these chapters by describing them as poetry or parable. However, the structure contains few of the features of such modes of Hebrew writing. It must be treated as historical truth.

There are, of course, different ways of telling history, but this passage is simple and precise, without elaboration or poetry. There is no trace of myth here either. It is straight narrative.

The structure of Genesis

Secondly, the structure of the book is clear to the careful reader. The book is broken down into many distinct sections, each identified with the statement, 'These are the generations of ..'.

Generations	Passage
Heavens & earth	1:1 — 2:4
Adam	2:5 — 5:2
Noah	5:3 — 6:9a
Sons of Noah	6:9b — 10:1
Sons of Shem	10:2 — 11:10a
Sons of Terah	11:10b — 11:27a
Sons of Ishamael & Isaac	11:27b — 25:19a
Sons of Esau & Jacob	25:19b — 37:2

Each section ends with the summary statement, 'These are the generations of ...'

Within these sections, there is a clear structure. There is a general survey of the descendants, starting with the 'least important' and then focusing on the specific line of interest (identifying the promised line through whom the Saviour would come). For example, considering the generations of Isaac, the record first describes the offspring of Esau and then concentrates on Jacob's. The first chapters are of identical form: the generations of the heavens and earth in general, climaxing with man's creation. Then the creation of man in detail is considered. Man is the centre of creation and the rest is subordinate in purpose to him (Genesis 2).

The perspective of the first two chapters is different. Chapter two focuses in on man, who is the climax of the first chapter. Chapter one is geocentric and, specifically, earth-centred. This is not a physical issue but spiritual. The earth was the centre of God's plan; the universe was subordinate. Man was the centre of God's plan for planet Earth; the geography, geology, biology *etc* are subordinate. We see that God's interest in the earth (and, indeed, of all creation) is centred on man's spiritual state (compare, for example, 2 Peter 3:5 and its context).

Days of Genesis 1

It is perhaps useful to summarize the chronological sequence given in Genesis 1. The creation of the heavens and the earth (v.1) is the beginning of time. God then began his activity of shaping and filling it for man:

> Day 1 : the creation of light in the midst of darkness.
> Day 2 : the creation of the sky and separation of the waters.
> Day 3 : the creation of land amidst the seas and the creation of seed-bearing plants.
> Day 4 : the creation of sun, moon and stars.
> Day 5 : the creation of sea creatures and birds.
> Day 6 : the creation of livestock, creeping creatures and wild animals. The creation of man and woman.

The Creation is summarized in terms of 'days'. For some reason, a lot of readers want to make this word possess anything but the obvious meaning! Typically, it is made to represent long periods of time: anything from a thousand years to millions! We need to remember that God is not constrained by time — not even by days! One might argue, why did he not work in an instant (rather than in 6 x 24 hour periods)? Even on this point the Bible gives us evidence. The creation week was designed as a model for man — six days work and one day rest (Exodus 20:11; 31:17; Hebrews 4:4). Man was created to work to that pattern. Failure to abide by it can be expected to cause unnecessary stress. (It is worth noting that, in Exodus 20:9-11, the same verb — *asah*, do/did — is used of man and God, emphasising the parallel application of the seven day week).

Another principle for the interpretation of the 'days' (or anything else in Scripture) is that the criterion must be biblical, even if it leaves us with unanswered questions and problems to be solved. (I am often amazed that the believer in creation is criticized for not being able to answer all the scientific implications, while the evolutionist — with his very much larger band of researchers — is expected to be allowed to wait for future discoveries!)

It is sometimes claimed that 'days' are used in Scripture to mean long periods of time. This is true (e.g. Genesis 2:4 uses 'day' to refer to the creation week). But, nowhere in Scripture (or elsewhere) is the structure 'evening and morning' and 'first day' etc. applied to anything except to genuine days (defined, of course, as here, by the earth's rotation about its axis).

Others have pointed to the statement that 'a day with the Lord is as a thousand years' (2 Peter 3:8). That too is true, but it proves too much! The text goes on to say 'and a thousand years as a day'. That would make the creation day equivalent to less than a quarter of a second! The point is simply that time is unimportant to God — he created it and he is not restricted by it.

Another interpretation is that the 'days' represent successive days of revelation. So, for example, on the first day, God revealed to Moses that he created the heavens and the earth and light. The next day, he told him about the creation of the atmosphere and distribution of the water. And so on. Though this is more consistent with the use of the word, one has to ask, Is it valid? Nowhere, here or elsewhere in Scripture, is this mode of delivery implied for the creation account. If God revealed things in this way (as in the book of Daniel, for example), the arrangement would be unambiguous. It would also be strange to reveal just a verse or two a day! The case is based on the argument that the Hebrew word *asah* can be translated 'showed' as well as 'made'. The case is weak in that, though it can be used this way for 'showed mercy,' it never means 'revealed'. The meaning is always consistent with the translation 'made' or 'did'. Again, the context is clear — the seventh day of rest is clearly *from the act* of creation, not its revelation (Genesis 2:2; Exodus 20:11).

In terms of the natural day, it is consistent with the observable facts. The life cycle of one plant often depends on another plant or animal. For example, the flowering plants depend on insects for pollination. What would have happened if a multi-thousand or multi-million year time lag occurred between the two?

Anyone who considers nature carefully will be impressed by its integration. There is a continuous chain, indeed, a complete cycle. This implies that creation took a short time. The psalmist notes, when referring to the creation of the heavens, 'For he spake and it was done; he commanded and it stood fast.' Instant creation is described.

Date of Creation

The other question to be considered at this point is, How long ago did this happen? It does not matter to the believer in Creation whether it was six thousand or six thousand million years ago. (To the evolutionist, even the latter time is far too short). But, we can ask, does the Bible give any clear indication?

The work of Ussher, who proposed that Creation occurred in 4004 BC, has often been criticized and ridiculed. Certainly he tried to prove too much detail from the Scripture record, but was he wrong *in principle?* The basis on which he worked was the Scriptural genealogies. If Genesis is historical, as we claim, then so are these. If they are not intended to be taken this way, then why all the detail about the ages of the men? What do the genealogies show? Using the Masoretic text (see the glossary in appendix D), we can generate a pattern such as shown in the figure 7.

Some claim that we cannot trust these genealogies too far, so let us consider a couple of their common arguments. It is pointed out that the genealogies may be incomplete. For example, Genesis 11:12 indicates that Arphaxad is the father of Salah, whereas Luke 3:36 says his son is Cainan; Salah was his grandson. (There is no distinction in the ancient language between son and grandson). So, it is concluded, accuracy was not important in these genealogies and they are probably full of such errors. If this were the case, then, of course, they would have no real meaning, yet they were obviously included for a purpose. However, even this example has no significance on the time interval — if Arphaxad begat Salah when he was thirty-five years of age, then he must have had his own son when he was about seventeen. The chronology is not affected.

Nor can we appeal to other texts such as the Samaritan and Septuagint texts (see the glossary for an explanation of these terms). They are often variable between their own copies and often inconsistent too. For example, some Septuagint versions have Methuselah living sixteen years after the Flood. This is impossible if only Noah's family survived. There is no good reason to reject the Masoretic text for these genealogies.

On the other hand, this Masoretic data is internally consistent. Note how (other than Noah and his sons), no-one lived after the Flood. That is consistent with the biblical record. So, while we may be the odd year out for some of the dates (because we do not know how fractional years were dealt with), it is clear that the biblical record implies that creation was just over six thousand years ago.

In later chapters, we will consider how this age ties in with geology. An example of the problem that 'old earth' believers are faced with (aside from the geological problems) is illustrated by the recent extraction of DNA from a fossilized magnolia leaf. This was in 'Miocene clay', the name given to a clay supposedly deposited

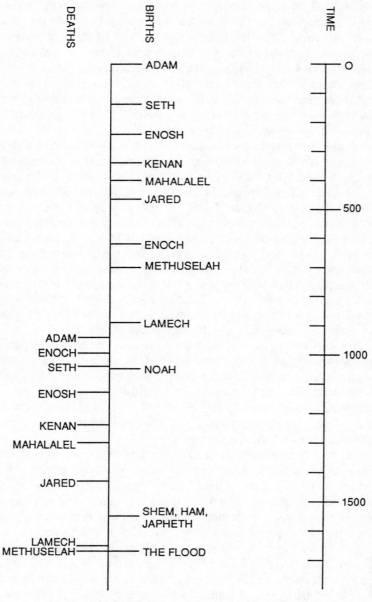

Figure 7: Time chart from Creation to the Flood.

about twenty million years ago. But, as any chemist would know, such a chemical could not last that long in the earth's climate (less than 10 000 years). (See also page 91).

A similar example relates to a protein extracted from the vertebrae of a fossilized dinosaur (a sauropod). This was found in the 'Jurassic rocks', supposedly 150 million years old. Again, it is highly improbable that such a substance could last that long.

Some have suggested that there could be a time gap between verses two and three of Genesis 1. Basically, the argument goes that God created the heavens and the earth and then there followed a seven day forming and filling of the earth. Until verse three, time would be irrelevant and so it could account for the large cosmological ages. While this is a possible interpretation, there is no reason (other than an accommodation to the proposed large ages) why the verses 1-2 should not be included in the first day of creation.

4.
Creation revealed

So, what does the biblical record tell us about God's creative activity? What did he do? It is well to remind ourselves that we cannot go back in time and see it. Nor can we repeat the experience. We *can* ask, What are the implications of the record? Can we observe these implications today?

Day one

On the first day, God tells us that he did two fundamental things — he created the 'heavens and the earth' and he created light. The planet was formed in space (as we now call it). At this stage (as confirmed by the subsequent record), the globe was 'without form and void'. This implies that it lacked its final structural and useful shape. (The 'formlessness' and 'emptiness' of 1:2 — *tohu* and *bohu* — is the same description as in Isaiah 34:11 and Jeremiah 4:23. The latter reference uses the same wording *tohu wabohu* to describe the reverse of creation, the act of judgment, and effectively expounds the wording in Genesis 1:2. It is a wasteness and emptiness as in a desert). It was empty of life.[1] The rest of the chapter describes the forming processes (days 1-3) and then the filling (days 4-6).

We will also notice that, over this week of activity, the work is 'worldwide'. We would expect, therefore, that these effects will be found all over the world. This is in contrast to modern geological activity which is localized. So, if we are to locate creation week work, it will be in world-wide structures.

We tend to think in terms of the sun as being *the* source of light. This verse tells us that light is a more fundamental property. This need not pose any problems for a scientist. Energy (which includes light) is a basic phenomenon. God filled the created order with this energy on the first day of creation. Of course, it was essential that this energy be available before the creation of life. Though we know that, the writer of Genesis would not appreciate such points unless they were revealed to him!

This light is clearly directional so that the rotating earth could be bathed in light and darkness alternately (to give the 'evening and the morning'). Though we now relate our day and night to the exposure to the sun and moon, that is not a necessary criterion: here the twenty-four hour day is related to this primeval light, not the light-bearers of Genesis 1:16.

This passage also draws attention, admittedly incidentally, to the fact that the universe is God-centred. Neither the sun, the earth or living things are divine. They were created. So, in these simple statements, we see too the undermining of false religion, both ancient and modern.

Day two

The second day saw the creation of 'the heavens' and the distribution of the waters below and above the sky. We can deduce that this action involved the establishment of the atmosphere surrounding the earth including its protective belts. These would need to be in place, of course, before life itself.

Furthermore, it is clear from the context that the original atmosphere was essentially the same as that experienced today. Those who believe that the world came into being through no-God, have to assume that the atmosphere contained no free oxygen (for example). That is, it was non-oxidising.[2] They have to resort to this conclusion because any chemicals required to produce the living cells would not survive in an oxidising environment without the process of life itself (this is why our bodies decay when life is taken from us). The evidence is that the atmosphere has always been oxidising, so creating another problem for those who wish to explain the origin of life by no-God.

The precise nature of the waters placed in the sky is a matter of debate. Obviously it includes the clouds and general water vapour in the atmosphere. Others consider that a more substantial water vapour canopy was involved. This would have a protective effect (for example, against harmful ultraviolet radiation) and would establish a uniform 'hot house'. It would also contribute to the deluge of Noah's day (see chapter 7). The earth was watered by dew or a mist, apparently not by rain (Genesis 2:6).

Day three

At this point, we have a globe covered with water and an atmosphere around it with some sort of water vapour cover. Light is provided by the energy (*'electromagnetic radiation'*) created on day one. The first work of day three was, therefore, to raise some of the solid crust of the earth above sea-level to form land. The land mass was separated from the waters, called seas; a boundary was set between them.

This, of course, implies a substantial geological disturbance in the raising of the rocks. Probably the effects of this would occur for a long time. Sediment would erode and settle for many years to come. This could mean that marine creatures could become trapped and fossilized in future years.

The 'Precambrian rocks' (the name given to the oldest group of rocks in the earth), are spread around the globe in a very uniform manner, as predicted, though, of course, disturbed by later geological activity. Though fossilization is rare in these layers, features such as the stromalites would be consistent with the effects of this third day activity. (Stromalites are layers of chalk-like material which are said to be the remains of microbiological organisms such as algae. There is considerable debate as to whether there is any evidence of an organic origin to these deposits. As one textbook of earth sciences puts it, 'Unfortunately, no micro-organisms have been detected'. So they could be inorganic deposits from this day's activity.)

Now the structure of the earth is in place, life can be formed. We are told that God formed all kinds of vegetation and fruit. Two new expressions are used at this point and repeated on later days. We are told that God looked on this work and appreciated it; it was *'good'*. It delighted him. The earth that had been without form and void was now an object of beauty. This word 'good' implies that it is in keeping with God's own nature -morally and aesthetically perfect;

Figure 8: The primary land mass: the original 'supercontinent'.

something of beauty. We can imagine the persons of the Trinity looking in delight on the work of Creation and agreeing among themselves, 'Yes, it is good'.

The Scriptures also record that, having created a variety of plants, he told them to reproduce, *each after its own kind*. We will see that his creative activity distinguished between plants, sea creatures, birds, wild and domesticated animals, creeping things and man. At each point we are given the same command (with a significant difference for man) to reproduce after their kind. Clearly there are boundaries within which they are commanded to reproduce, that is, *after their own kind*.

Though an exact scientific term to identify 'kinds' does not seem to be available, it has a clear biblical distinction: it is defined by a reproductive barrier. (The nearest general equivalent to the 'kind' is the biological category of a 'family,' but an exact match is unlikely). The 'kind' would not generate offspring with something of another kind. This, of course, means that we can have a general category 'dog' which will include all the different breeds we are acquainted with today. But, they will be distinct from the 'cat' kind. We are not told how many different 'breeds' of dog were made on day six, nor, of course, how many dogs themselves were created. It is possible (and generally believed in terms of the biblical context and scientific observations) that God would have created an original dog kind, for example, and that it would have contained the genetic potential for a variety of breeds — short and long ears, large or small bodies, different coat lengths, different colours, etc. This is in keeping with practical observations that a specific plant or animal still has genetic potential for a range of varieties.

Again, we can see that our observations in nature accord with the biblical record. The Creation account makes it clear that, from the beginning, there was a 'forest' of variety of life in both the fauna and flora. Though further development within families of animals (for example, to give the different breeds of dogs) was to occur, the full range of life is present and complete. This is in contrast to the philosophy of those who consider a no-God process starting with one simple cell which gradually branches out over millions of years to give variety. This latter process is often pictured as a tree (*phylogenetic tree*). As the fossil record shows, this is a false picture of what happened. There has always been variety with the flora and fauna existing from the first in their modern forms.

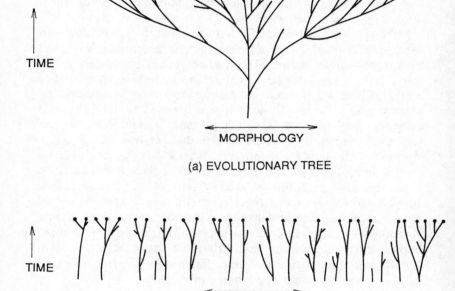

TIME

MORPHOLOGY

(a) EVOLUTIONARY TREE

TIME

MORPHOLOGY

(b) CREATIONIST ORCHARD

**Figure 9: A comparison of evolutionary and creationist interpretations of
the origin and development of living forms
(Asterisk represents currently observed species).**

How did one pair of animals generate such a variety? For example, God *may* have caused it to happen by creating a number of animals of the same kind and yet with some genetic difference. Inter-breeding would then produce variety. (Man's variety has, of course, resulted from a single pair).

The figure 10 shows how a variety of observed examples can arise from a limited gene pool. Incredibly large variations can arise from a more extensive range of genetic information: all without generating new information. In fact, experience shows that it is extremely difficult to generate new, useful, non-lethal genetic information. It is more likely that genetic information will be lost, rather than spontaneously generating new information. For example, in the diagram, if the white offspring were isolated from the rest, then its offspring could not contain the gene for producing red skin and so that genetic trait would be lost.

Another *possible* cause of variety (especially after the Flood) could be environmental factors. A recent example of this effect concerned rabbits found in Australia. These have descended from one European species and yet, in hot areas, they have long ears whereas those from cold regions have short ears. Researchers experimented with both groups at different laboratory temperatures. There was a reversion by each group to that indicated by the natural environment. New genetic information was not produced, but (it would seem) the temperature control selected which genetic trait was produced. Similar temperature effects have been observed in the selection of the sex of offspring of some animals.

There is an interesting moral implication that must be considered. If God set these boundaries, with this restrictive command on reproduction, is it permissible to carry out experiments which try cross-breeding animals which are clearly of different kinds?

Day four

On the fourth day of creation, God filled the heavens with the 'heavenly bodies' — the sun, moon and stars specifically being identified. Again, notice that these were created specifically for life on the earth — to provide light for day and night, to determine the time periods, and so on. From early days, man has been impressed with these early time-pieces and their regular actions.

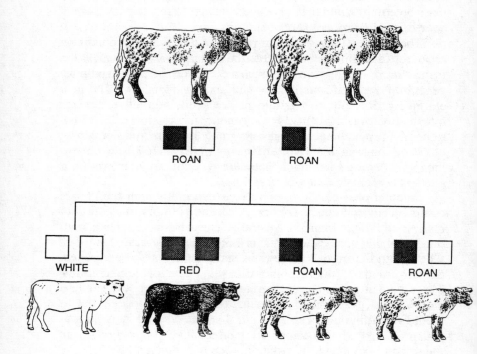

Figure 10: Colour genetics of shorthorn cattle.
One can observe three colours: white, red and roan (mixed colouring). The diagram shows the possible outcomes of the mating of two roan cattle. Each has a red gene and a white gene, one of which will be passed onto the offspring. If the offspring is white and isolated from the rest, the red gene is lost.

The light that was non-specific in origin (from day 1) is now to be localized in these heavenly bodies. We do not know (because we are not told) how the light from distant stars could be seen on a young earth. They are so far away that it may take thousands of millions of years to reach us under normal circumstances. We can speculate on possible answers, but we do know that such a problem to us is no problem to an almighty God. He is the Creator of time as well as the stars. Maybe one day we will have a confident answer; maybe we will not. In any case, we live by faith, not by sight.

In considering such problems, we need to be clear that the Creation week is not claiming to be a record of normal science, but of God's miraculous, unrepeated (and, by man, unrepeatable) activity. This is clear by a consideration of every aspect of science. Obviously normal biological processes are not described (animals *etc* were created not regenerated); normal chemical processes for the production of the chemicals of the cells are not applicable; the normal physical laws are not appropriate (as in the generation of instant star light on the earth). Normal "science" does not begin until the end of the creation week. (It is interesting to note that concepts like the Big Bang Theory, which is devised as a no-God process for the beginning of the universe, also have to consider processes beyond the present natural laws.)

Days five and six

On the fifth day, God filled the sea with life and the air with birds. He commanded them to be fruitful and multiply to fill the earth. Similarly, on day six, he created domesticated animals, creeping things and wild animals. Again, he was pleased with what he saw.

At the most basic level, this chapter teaches that God was the Creator of all things and that each category of life was deliberately made. There are clear distinctions between each category. Any explanation of origins that ignores these parameters is unbiblical.

There is another interesting implication of this passage. If all life were created by God in one week, then there is no kind of animal that has not, at some time, co-existed with man! This conflicts with the popular view of this history of the earth, but we believe it is in keeping with the observable evidence. It will be discussed further in chapter 7.

There can be no doubt that the clear message of this great passage is that God created each living thing in full working order. So, each cell was complete and fully functioning. Now this too is an interesting point which accords with what we observe in nature and in the laboratory. We noted earlier in the chapter that the chemicals needed to produce a living organism are, of themselves, unstable in the modern oxidising atmosphere. Since the evidence (from the Bible and from observation) is that the atmosphere on the earth has always been oxidising, it is clear that the chemicals had to be a part of the living cell from the start. They would not have lasted long enough to come together by chance.

We can take this further. The living cell is not stable alone either. It decays rapidly. Perhaps the most dramatic demonstration of this is in the passage concerning the death of Lazarus. Martha and Mary protested (quite reasonably) that after four days in the tomb, he would stink from the decay. Cells only survive (until they have generated their own replacement cells) in a fully living system.

Another interesting aspect of the importance of the created living organism is found in the structural nature of many of the chemicals that are involved in the metabolism. Many of these compounds (for example, the *amino acids* and *sugars*) can occur in two different forms. They are often likened by chemists to human hands: there is a right-handed form and a left-handed form. Any chemical process used in the laboratory to synthesize these substances yields a mixture of the two. It cannot be avoided. Strangely, in living systems, only one form of each of these compounds is generated: left-handed amino acids and right-handed sugars. This can only occur in a living system.

The structures of the cellular materials are even more complicated. Proteins are made up from the amino acids. Proteins are the active components of many parts of the living organism: for example, the hair, the muscles, the skin, the enzymes and so on. The property of the protein is determined by the structure. This is affected by the sequence of amino acids. There are twenty different amino acids that are available in nature. Every protein has a specific sequence of these. Most sequences generate ineffective proteins. The chances of getting a meaningful protein of one hundred units, which is the shortest likely structure, from a random grouping of these units is calculated as 10^{70} to 1 against. The number is massive and hard to visualize: it is the number 1 followed by 70 zeros (just

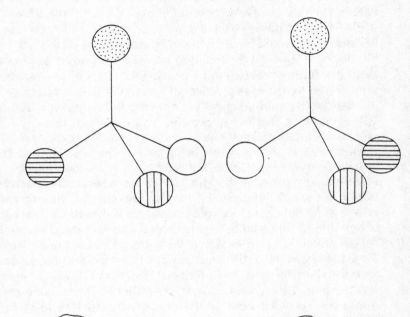

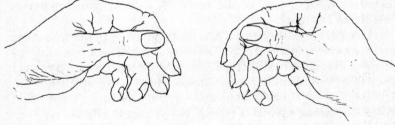

Figure 11: Right and left-handed chemicals.
Just as gloves are not super-imposable and cannot be put on the 'wrong' hands, so some chemicals are non-super-imposable and the alternative form cannot be used in a living system (The differently shaded spheres represent different groups of atoms).

as 10^6 is 1 followed by six zeros, that is 1000000, a million). Some chemists have proposed even larger values than this. In fact, we have to say that there are not enough atoms available in the universe to enable a non-directed process to sample all of these forms. (Even if it did, it would not know that a *successful* form had been found because there would be no living organism yet to identify it!)

Suppose a way were found to produce the correct sequence, there is a further problem to be faced. This chain of one hundred units can be folded up in a variety of ways. Again, in practice, only one way is effective biologically. To deviate from this *conformation* will result in an ineffective protein. An example of this is in the enzymes which are important to every process in the living cell: respiration and digestion just being two of the best known. The enzyme is a large molecule, but only one site on the molecule is effective. Any change in the structure causes a loss in its effectiveness. (This was demonstrated in the previous chapter when considering haemoglobin, for example). Now here is the crunch: there are about 10^{80} (1 followed by eighty zeros!) conformations available for our protein! Even if we accept the conventional age of the earth, there have been only 10^{17} (one hundred thousand million million) seconds since the earth was formed. If our non-directed system could explore 10^{15} (a thousand million million) different conformations every second it would still not have sufficient time to explore them all. It all speaks of the work of a Great and Supremely Intelligent Designer.

It is still easy to underestimate the complexity of the cell! It has been calculated that there are 239 protein molecules in a minimal cell. For the cell to be fully functioning, *all* these have to be present simultaneously. The chances against this happening are 10^{119850} to 1. Such figures are ridiculous and defy any chance of a no-God process constructing such a system. No wonder the Bible says 'The fool has said in his heart, "There is no God."' (Psalm 53:1). By the way, these calculations are concerned with just one group of substances the proteins; there are many more!

The earth was a planet now filled with life in ecological balance and in beauty. The scene was set for his ultimate purpose in all this work — the human being. It was mankind that God purposed to create. It was for mankind that God designed the world. So, on the sixth day, he made the animals. He also created man and woman, the climax and purpose of Creation.

References

1. W W Fields, 'Unformed and Unfilled,' Presbyterian & Reformed Publishing, New Jersey, 1978.
2. J H J Peet, 'Chemical Evolution — Some Difficulties,' Faith and Thought, 1982, 109(2), 127-154.

5.
Mankind, in God's image

The creation of man was similar to and yet different from that of the rest of creation. It was similar in that it was at God's command. It was also the creation of a separate group of creatures, distinct from what had gone before. Genesis 2 emphasizes that man was created from the dust of the ground, not from previous living creatures and that woman was made from man. The wording is unique in the case of man. Of the plants and animals, he said, 'Let the earth bring forth ...' *but* for man, he said, 'Let us make man ...'

The basic distinction is in what God said about man's creation: 'Let us make man *in our image*'. So, it was in God's image that man was made. The animals were each the first of their kind and reproduction was after *their own kind*. Adam, however, was a 'son of God' (Luke 3:38) — he was made after God's likeness. It was God's intention that man would reproduce after *his* own likeness. Of no other creature was this true. We would, therefore, expect to find that man was in some way, or ways, fundamentally different from the rest of creation and also that he was, in some way or ways, like God. Paul used this argument to demonstrate man's stupidity in worshipping the figment of his own imagination rather than his own Creator (Acts 17:28-29).

Image and likeness

The complementary words 'image' and 'likeness' are used to emphasize meaning and to avoid any ambiguity. It is probable that we should see 'likeness' as being used in a more limited sense.

Mankind was made — and still is, within the limits described below
— in the 'image of God'. This refers to those characteristics that
make him human and so distinctive from the rest of creation. To be
described as being in the 'likeness of God' is to state the spiritual
relationship between man and God. The perfection relates to those
with a godly heart. The expression 'likeness' is used again of our
Lord Jesus and his coming in the likeness of sinful man (Romans
8:3). Just as Christ was *not* a sinful man, so we are not God. Christ
himself is described as the 'image of the invisible God' (Colossians
1:15; see also John 1:14, Hebrews 1:3). The word means that we
bear a reproduction of some of God's characteristics. As Sinclair
Ferguson points out[1], these terms are synonymous with the expression, 'son of ..'. (Genesis 5:3). As this writer also aptly put it, 'He
does not want hired servants (he has angels enough!); he wants
children'.

Often there is confusion over the idea that human beings are
partly physical and clearly God is Spirit only. First of all, we must
not confuse 'image and likeness' with 'identity'. Nor must we
ignore the physical aspect of mankind. He is physical and spiritual
and we must not separate the two here to get round the confusion.
Man was made in the image of God — and that must imply his whole
being. The human's physical faculties are demonstrations of God's
spiritual ones. We have the same problem with the
anthropomorphic terms applied to God: his hands, eye, and so on.
We must remember that God is not made in man's image, but the
other way round. Our physical hands (*etc.*) are made to do as God's
spiritual hands (and on a more finite scale).

Similarly, we live in days in which there is confusion over the
sex of God. But this is because we assume that God is made in the
likeness of mankind — and often this is the god that these
theologians worship, a mental idol of their own making. God is
Father; Christ is his Son. These are not flexible options. Mankind,
however, was made in God's likeness and our fatherhood and
sonship are a pale reflection of theirs. Woman was made for man,
and she too is in the image of God. The spiritual parallel is the
church, the bride of Christ.

As we will see, the Bible tells us that man fell from the state in
which God had created him, so falling short of his glory (Romans
1:21-23; 3:23). But, the work of the Holy Spirit in the Christian is

to reform the person to the likeness of Christ (Romans 8:28-29; 1 Corinthians 15:49).

Man's creation was from the dust of the earth *and* by the hand and the breath of God. Since a human being returns to the dust and cannot rise from it, this indicates the impotency of the dust alone. We live because of God's work in us. The description that God 'formed' man (Genesis 2:7) is that used of the potter who forms a vessel from the clay. We also note that this creative work was from the non-living dust: not previous animals or 'lesser humans'. Adam's origin is miraculous and special.

It is clear from this account that all people have the same common ancestor: Adam. (Indeed, we are all descended from Noah too). So, there is no distinction due to race, colour, *etc*. None is inferior or superior. There is no 'master race' or 'slave race'. While every individual is different, all come from the same original genetic stock (Acts 17:26). The genetic variation between the races is small. For example, the skin colour is probably defined by no more than ten genes. The differences certainly do not warrant any concept of one race being superior to another.

Human uniqueness

Linnaeus, a Christian biologist renowned for his classification system, effectively summarized man as a unique mammal in six respects: theological, moral, natural, physiological, dietetic (that is, with respect to diet) and pathological. In each of these areas, man is significantly different even from the other mammals.

The distinction between mankind and the rest of creation is emphasized in the table which lists some of the unique features of humans, compared, for example, to the most similar animal, the ape. Though, of course, God is spirit and so the physical features cannot, of themselves, be said to be in his likeness, they are the means by which those unique attributes of God are communicated in people.

Figure 12: Man — in whose image?

The uniqueness of mankind

Posture	upright
Creativity	use and construction of tools construction of complex structures artistic ability
Communication	use of many languages variety of means of communication: word (prose & poetry), laughter, music, body language, etc. unique sense of family relationships & loyalty
Intelligence	accumulation of knowledge ability to count to large numbers mathematical ability capability of complex reasoning & abstract thought lateral thinking development of theories judging planning
Morality	appreciation of good and evil conscience ethical responsibility respect for life spiritual dimension powers of awe, worship & self-sacrifice ability of morality to overcome environmental influences

Genesis 1 is concerned with the activity of God in creation. We would expect, therefore, that mankind would also display this creative ability. The work of creation *ex nihilo* (from nothing) must be a unique work of God, but human beings are creative in the abstract sphere — they can use their minds to design or to develop logical arguments. They can create music, art, tools, machines and so on. It is not the use of simple tools that is the criterion — some animals have that ability — but the design of tools, particularly those with symmetry which is characteristic.

God's creative work is by communication, 'God said..'. When creating man, we read of communication within the Godhead, 'Let us ..'. People are unique in the depth and breadth of their communication skills. Humans are able to reason, debate, discuss, encourage, persuade, *etc.* Mankind has both the ability to communicate and a message to communicate. We see man using this facility immediately after his creation when God tells him to name the animals (Genesis 2:19-20). This command covers the 'beasts of the field,' the 'birds of the air' and 'cattle'. It excludes the fish, creeping things (reptiles, amphibia, insects, *etc.*). This probably means that the categories are more limited than those of Genesis 1:24, covering those kinds with which man would normally come into contact (the 'domesticated animals').

There is an interesting description of our ability to communicate given in the scriptures. For example, in Psalm 108:1, the passage is rendered (in the King James version), 'I will sing and give praise, even with my glory.' Other references include Psalm 30:12, 57:8. The same word, 'glory', is used in Psalm 19:1. The key to interpreting this is Psalm 16:9 which is applied to Christ in Acts 2:26, where it is rendered 'tongue'. So, our ability to use our tongues to the praise of God becomes our glory. It demonstrates again that we are made in the image of our Creator.

Human authority

When God made man, he said, 'Let him have dominion ..'. He was given dominion over all of creation. As God is sovereign, so man, in a more limited sphere, is also king. God made him lord over the created sphere. This was not an abdication of God's sovereignty; man is responsible to God. His dominion is not one of tyranny or of exploitation. That would not be the biblical understanding of authority. Psalm 72 described the dominion of the king (ultimately, of the King of kings) over a vast sphere. But the context is clear: it is one of care. Man's dominion over the created order is a rule of care. Man is told to tend the world God has made. He has a responsibility to care, develop and cultivate. It is a position of service and stewardship (and so, accountability). These things belong to God: 'To the Lord your God belong the heavens, even the highest heavens, the earth and everything in it' (Deuteronomy 10:14). They are not ours to exploit.

Man is not an absolute sovereign. He is finite and completely dependent on the power and will of the infinite Creator. (This, in turn, means that man's will is only truly free when it is in harmony with the will of God). Only God has the right to destroy this earth, which he will do in judgment. That right is not delegated to us. Indeed, it is because of our sin that the earth is under the judgment of God (see the next chapter).

Human intelligence

Human intelligence is unique in the created order. Though most people recognize that mankind is the 'crown' of the natural system, they often find it difficult to understand why a person is inferior to many animals in his or her defence system. The ape can out-manoeuvre a human being in his speed and strength. (This is contrary to any evolutionary prediction!) Mankind's defence is based on his intelligence — he can outwit the animal by the use of his mind — not on any evolved physical capability. Human beings are the only creatures that have developed a technology that can change their way of life.

We see man created as intelligent — from the beginning. He is described as having the ability to reason (e.g. Genesis 1:28; 2:16-17; 2:19-20). The first men were able to produce fire (Genesis 4:4-5), cultivate crops and shepherd domesticated animals (Genesis 4:2). From the beginning he had a complete language (2:9) and soon learnt to use fibrous plants and weave material into tents (4:20). Quickly he learnt how to construct musical instruments and compose music (4:21) and then engaged in sophisticated metallurgy (4:22). All this took place within the life-time of Adam. It is a myth that early man ('Stone Age' or earlier) was less intelligent than his modern descendents.

The mind of mankind is many orders of magnitude above that of the animal kingdom. This is again to be expected from the biblical record that man was made in the image of God. If the process of man's origin were that of no-God, how do we account for this remarkable feature? Professor Paul Davies stated this plainly.[2] He points out that man's intellectual powers, which enable him to explore the world, are 'deeply puzzling'. He finds it difficult to believe that our ability to engage in scientific research is an accident of our evolutionary descent. He believes that the complexity of the mind demonstrates that there is a fundamental link between its structure and the natural laws that scientists seek to study. Mankind is a self-conscious creature. He knows that he knows something — in contrast to a computer (1 Corinthians 2:11).

We assume that a human being's reasoning powers are reliable. This, again, is an obvious result of the work of a wise Creator. But if no design was involved, how can the mind be relied on? How, for example, can we rely on its reasoning for the origin of life by a no-God process? It is a logical trap. Mankind makes himself foolish in his attempts to exclude the Creator.

Human behaviour, in contrast to the animal's, is non-instinctive and so has unlimited variety. Before the Fall corrupted the moral nature of the human kind, this meant that numerous courses of action were open to him, all of them wholesome and good. Man is able to plan and to foresee the consequences of his behaviour, so adapting his plans accordingly. He can ignore experience if he so desires. He is characterized by his ability to organize. He can invent mathematics and follow complicated abstract reasoning.

Human relationships

The uniqueness of people, compared to the animals, is also notable in the sexual relationships. This undoubtedly arises from the creation order in which God made man and woman both in the image of God (so neither is inferior) and to complement each other in love. As Matthew Henry wrote in his commentary on Genesis, '[She was] not made from his head to top him, not out of his feet to be trampled on by him, but out of his side to be equal with him, under his arm to be protected, and near his heart to be beloved.'

When Adam was created and given mastery over the animals, God noted that there was nothing to meet his need for companionship (Genesis 2:20). Adam could call them, but he could not converse with them. So God made woman: a very special mate. Neither is complete without the other. The glory of the woman is that man is incomplete without her.

Adam and Eve were made separately but one was also made from the other to emphasize their complementarity. To complement each other, man and woman must be different even though equal. Any modern attempt to suppress the differences does an injustice to each and is unscriptural. The creation of woman as a 'helper' (*ezer*, 2:8,10) does not imply inferiority or subordination. It is used of an ally in war (1 Kings 20:16). The word is used of God too (Psalm 115:9-11)! The relationship emphasized in Ephesians 5 is one of unlimited commitment: the man is to love his wife, even to die for her; the woman's response is to submit herself to that love and care. Mating and breeding are not synonymous in man as they are in animals: love and self-sacrifice are the keys. A simple but significant comment (that is, in the light of later events) is the statement at the end of Genesis 2: they were naked but unashamed. There was no shame in this relationship.

The roles of a man and a woman are made plain in Scripture (e.g. Genesis 3:16; 1 Corinthians 11:3,9). Man is in a position of leadership: that is a role of protection, support, *etc*. It is a position of sacrifice, *not* superiority. It refers to function. John Benton, in a sermon, has given a helpful definition of leadership on the basis of the biblical principles. In the partnership of two equals before God, man and woman, the man bears the primary responsibility before God to lovingly protect and sacrificially lead the relationship in the direction of God's glory and the woman's good. The fact that woman was made from man *and* man is born from woman emphasizes their mutual dependence. There is an equality in creation (both are made in the image of God) and in salvation (Galatians 3:28; 1 Peter 3:7).

Mankind has freedom from the rigorous chemical control of the reproductive functions, whereas animals are constrained by these periodic functions. Human beings, on the other hand, are essentially free to mate at any time of the year, responding to love rather than simple chemical or environmental factors. The role of people in the care of the offspring is unique in creation. The family unit in animals is relatively superficial; in humans it is for a lifetime and over great distances.

Human posture

The obvious visual difference between humans and the animals is in posture. This is critical. Many of the features already noted are dependent on this posture. When age or sickness cause a bending of the spine, other abilities become frustrated.

The fore-limbs are freed because of the posture making them available for manipulative action. The relative size of the upper and lower limbs is the reverse of that found in apes. The hand of a person is critical in design for power, for the ability to hold, pull, construct, *etc*. There is a nervous connection between the hand and the brain that results in the brilliant coordination of, for example, the concert pianist.

The human vertebral column has a complex curvature — it is neither perfectly straight nor uniformly curved. This aids the flexibility of the body and enables the person to stand truly upright. The upright human posture enables us to look up as well as forward and down, giving a broad range of vision. It enables face-to-face communication with hand and facial gestures to reinforce the verbal expressions. Mankind's ability to speak is affected by his erect posture. This permits a critical configuration of the wind-pipe and vocal organs, without the need to change the normal head position. Many animals have to change the head position in order to make a vocal noise (for example, a dog has to change its head position when it barks).

Professor Verna Wright has pointed out that a popular myth is that man frequently suffers back problems such as slipped discs because of his upright posture. He demonstrates that there is no relationship between the two and that such complaints are to be found in the animal kingdom too, where they can be more profound.

The most notable aspect of a human being, marking him out as different from the animals, is in the spiritual realm. We are spiritual beings. We have the ability to worship God. We can pray to him (Genesis 3:8). We can read his Word. We can write hymns of praise. We have the potential to enjoy him for ever.

Those who reject man's origins as being by special and specific creation by God, believe that his closest relative is the ape. We have seen that there are significant differences between the two kinds. In contrast, the Bible says that man was made in the image of God and the observable evidence supports this. As James Kelso has aptly expressed it, 'Man's closest relative is God.'

We note also that God commanded that the animals and humans

could eat plants for food. The freedom of mankind to eat meat came later, but we need to appreciate that this later change did not take God by surprise. He knew the future and created us with the ability to live not only on a vegetarian diet but with a meat one.

Day seven

God looked on his work now and saw that it was not just 'good' but 'very good'. With Adam and Eve in place, God was satisfied with all that he had done and rested from the work of creation. The seventh day of the week was the first day after the completion of his creative activity. It was to be a day of rest for man and woman too. In their case, it is a necessary time for restoration from work. God did not need to have a time of restoration, of course. In fact, he was and is still active in sustaining the world.

Because man was made in God's image, he is special. He has worth — worth above the animals. Every human — male and female — must be treated with respect. There are no second-class citizens: we are all first-class. We must not differentiate between people. Though some may deserve special respect because of age or authority, no one should be despised or considered unimportant. All should be loved and respected. Life itself is precious and should not be taken (Genesis 9:5-6) by deliberate action or by reckless behaviour.

Before we leave the Creation week, we must note an important point. The work of creation is specifically stated to be 'finished' (Genesis 2:2). This is confirmed by Paul's use of the past perfect tense (Colossians 1:16-17). This passage makes it clear that, in the past, Christ created all things, but now, in the present, that same power is used to uphold all things. There is a clear contrast here to any sense that new kinds of animals are being formed. And that is consistent with our observation and experimentation.

References

1. Sinclair Ferguson, 'Children of the Living God,' Banner of Truth, 1989.
2. Paul Davies, Daily Telegraph, 1992, March 2nd.

6.
Ruined by the fall

The fall of man into sin also had a significant effect on creation. Because Adam was the federal head (the legal representative of all mankind), his sin affected the whole of creation. That which was in harmony now groans waiting for its redemption (Romans 8:22). In particular, men and women are now conceived in sin (Psalm 51:5).

God made it easy for man to obey him. He placed him in a garden full of fruit and told him that he could eat freely from any of these trees except that of the Tree of the Knowledge of Good and Evil. One tree out of a huge orchard! But man disobeyed.

An early Roman Christian, Tertullian, said, 'We must not consider merely by whom all things were made, but by whom they were perverted'. There are two answers to this: Satan and Adam. Though Satan was responsible for the temptation, Adam was guilty of listening to, and believing, his lie, given through Adam's wife, Eve.

A number of consequences of the Fall are highlighted in Genesis 3. The nakedness which displayed an open-ness and purity in the garden became an embarrassment. This is not described in terms of public contact (because there were no other people at this time), but between a man and his wife! The beautiful relationship was tarnished.

Satan had used a creature as his vehicle to tempt mankind. Obviously in the perfection of Eden, this serpent was not frightening and may even have been considered fascinating and beautiful. Few people have a lack of fear when they meet a snake now! There was apparently an anatomical change in this creature too — it was to creep on its belly and eat earth rather than vegetation. It has been noted that many snakes have rudimentary limbs and it is tempting to connect the two facts.

For the woman, a specific judgment was given. She was to find childbirth, though something fulfilling and exciting, an experience of enhanced pain. Her relationship to her husband was also affected. Man and woman had been created in beautiful complementarity, as lords of the creation. As a result of sin, man's authority over woman was to become intimidating. (This is a statement of fact, not a command that man is to behave in this way. The Christian approach — see chapter 5 — is very different: it is not intimidating). The same expression is used in Genesis 4:7, 'its desire is for you'. The meaning in this latter reference is that Cain is a slave to sin's desire. The will of the woman is brought into subjection to that of her husband. Eve had sought to rule Adam by giving him the forbidden fruit, attempting to usurp God's law; now Adam was to rule her. Man's original authority was for her blessing; his love was unspoilt. Here, love becomes lust; responsibility to care becomes a desire to dominate. Control now moves from gentle love and care to instinctive urges. The pull of sin is in a downward direction. There is a sinful inclination towards an abuse of authority. The passage does not claim a *superiority* of man over woman. It refers to function. The Lord knew the chaos that sin would bring to relationships. An established order was necessary. Paul emphasizes the mutual dependency of man and woman (1 Corinthians 11:11-12).

Man had been made in the image of God (Genesis 5:1). Now he would reproduce 'in his own image'. (Genesis 5:3) This speaks against the priority given by some to the 'universal Fatherhood of God'. Now it is by redemption, not by physical reproduction, that we become the 'sons of God' (John 1:12).

Mankind is still human; the image of God, though defaced, remains. Indeed, this is clearly stated (Genesis 9:6). But, 'all have sinned and come short of the glory of God' (Romans 3:23). The image is tarnished. When he looks into a mirror, as it were, he sees a distorted image. So, his creativity can lead to perversity and destruction. His intelligence can cause him to convince himself that there is no God and so God calls him, 'Fool' (Psalm 53:1). His dominion leads to tyranny.

Mankind had been created to work, to exercise dominion after the model of his Creator (that is, management and care). Because of his rebellion, however, the ground was to change. He would have to labour against the rebellion of 'thorns and thistles'. It is not clear whether these were a new creation or a change in the properties of existing plants. Just as man experienced changes physically, so the effect on plants could be a change in the characteristics.

Origin of human death

Perhaps the most striking physical change was death, the promised punishment for sin. Clearly this is not only spiritual death, but physical. Just as man had been made of the dust of the earth, so he would return to it (Genesis 3:19). His only salvation would come through the death and resurrection of the last Adam (Romans 5:14-15; 1 Corinthians 15:44-47). 'Christ died for our sins'. Consequently, the sting of death is gone —Christ removes us from the world of sin to the presence of God.

Paul told Timothy that everything was created 'good' (1 Timothy 4:4). But, death came through man (1 Corinthians 15:21) and so decay (Romans 8:20-21). These are not a part of the natural order, as is a necessary belief of those who seek a process of evolution. These references show that death was not a part of God's 'good' order (see also 1 Corinthians 15:26: death is an enemy).

Ecclesiastes 12:7 makes it clear that as the body returns to dust, the spirit returns to God. Man is accountable to his Creator.

Adam and Eve had enjoyed intimate fellowship with God. They walked and talked together in the garden. Now mankind was banished from God's presence. Though God would speak to humans again, occasionally and directly, it was to be a rare event. As the federal head, Adam's sin passed on all people. By nature, all men are now sinners. We sin because this is our nature (that is, we are sinners already and not because we sin; our behaviour is the result of our nature, not the reverse).

The Bible record from this point is one of degeneration, physically and morally. Sickness arose. This implies the origin of viruses at this point. They have a symbiotic relationship to living things and cannot multiply without them. Of course, this relationship may have been suppressed in some way up to this point, or may have been ineffective until the Lord brought about certain physiological changes in mankind. In the same way, though some bacteria have beneficial properties, some changes may have occurred in existing ones to make them harmful. Whatever the explanation of the detail, things became very different for human beings now.

Mutations

Again, this is in keeping with our experience. Changes do occur in genetic information (that is, hereditary information held in the genes; see the glossary). We call these changes *mutations*. These have been found to have assorted implications: some (though very few) may have apparently beneficial features, most would seem to be neutral, but there are often harmful, even lethal, effects. For example, the change of one item in nine hundred in the genetic information for the human haemoglobin can lead to the fatal sickle cell anaemia. Mutations occur in organisms that are already adapted to their enviroment, so they are most likely to be deleterious. They are a source of degeneration. They may result in a loss of eyes, but not in their production.

Two points should be noted. Firstly, the limits of genetic change already referred to are not breached. There have been no crossings of the boundaries between the kinds as a result of mutations. A fruit fly is still a fruit fly; a dog is still a dog and so on. Secondly, no new extra information is generated. The old is changed, but nothing new is produced. No new organs are formed. Evolutionary progression requires the generation of new genetic information, over and above that originally present, and that on a massive scale. Such a change has never been observed.

The fruit fly, *drosophila*, has been extensively studied for mutational effects. It is suitable for study because of its short generation time, so the effect of the transmission to the offspring can be measured. Many effects have been observed resulting, for example, in many different degrees of wing damage. The fly is disadvantaged by the mutations. Certainly, though, it is still a fruit fly. It has also been observed that the cell checks replicated information and corrects it. As an example, de Beers has reported that a blind mutation in the *drosophila* is corrected in ten generations, leading to recovered sight.[1]

The existence of these boundaries in mutational change is further demonstrated by the work of the Russian scientist, Dmitri

Kouznetsov. He found that if a modified gene is produced, regardless of its potential usefulness, it will not be expressed as a protein. The translation of the genetic information into a protein requires a group of substances in the cytoplasm (see the glossary) which are, in fact, powerful inhibitors of any change in the genes. It would appear that the Lord has imposed boundaries that cannot be crossed. The action of genes is regulated by complementary genes. This creates another control to the development of new genes. It is possible that the different kinds of animals are characterized by different regulatory mechanisms and these represent the boundaries.

The genes are packed with information. They contain instructions for the construction of every part of the organism (with the possible variations of colour, size, *etc*). Mutations are the result of sin — but they do not disguise the handiwork of the Creator. A parallel situation is a piece of paper with writing on it being left in the rain. The writing gets washed and spoilt, but, if we know the concepts behind it (for example, the original language), we can decode it. Similarly we can often take spoilt genetic information and determine what it should have been but for the damage. This is illustrated by medical research which involves the study of genetic information to determine the causes of disease.

The Fall has had a dramatic and serious effect on the creation. It leads to alienation, suffering, frustration, pain, decay and sorrow. Degeneration from the perfection of creation is the keynote.

The effect of human sin on the natural order is well illustrated in Hosea 4:1-3. Because of our rejection of God's standards, the land was a victim. As William Badke outlines in 'Project Earth'[2], it is not just a matter of people spoiling the world because of their bad conduct, but the earth is positively subjected to judgment by God: 'God became a defiler of the earth. He turned round and attacked the creation he had so lovingly formed, diminishing its witnesses both to his glory and to his power to nurture'. God cursed the ground (Genesis 3:17) and, as we shall see, he destroyed what he had created (Genesis 6:7). Just as the creation was a God-directed process, so was the judgment. Neither represents a no-God process.

We inherit Adam's sinful nature: that's a spiritual, rather than genetic effect. Mankind is a spiritual being as well as a physical being.

Because the Fall brought a change in human nature, our nature needs to be changed again. The Law can only demonstrate our fallen nature (Romans 3:20). We need a rebirth (John 3:3). We need to be a new creation (2 Corinthians 5:17). Indeed, the whole of creation looks for a renewal (Romans 8:20-21). As it was created by God, so it needs to be recreated by him.

References

1. G de Beer, 'Homology, the unsolved problem'. Oxford, 1971.
2. W B Badke, 'Project Earth,' Multnomah Press, 1991; pp. 54-55.

7.
Destruction by the flood

Genesis 4 tells us of the sons of Adam and the first murder, by Cain of his brother, Abel. For this, Cain and his descendants were banished from the presence of the Lord (Genesis 4:16) This line was clearly an ungodly one. God blessed Adam and Eve with another son to replace Abel; this was Seth. The implication of Genesis 4:16 is that, although Adam and his family were banished from Eden, in some special way, God was still with them, in a way that he was not with Cain. This is borne out by such godly men as Enoch and Noah, for example.

Genesis 5 gives us historical data on Adam's descendants. These were people of extraordinary longevity. Though some try to explain it away, we have no problem in accepting this record. Indeed, we would say, 'Why not'? Had Adam not sinned, mankind would not have died. Had Adam not sinned, disease and ageing would not have occurred. Some have suggested reducing the large ages by a factor (for example, dividing them all by ten) to get 'more meaningful' ages, but that does not work: it gives meaningless ages for the ages of the fathers at the birth of their firstborn! If we do not accept this record as fact, we are going to have serious problems with Genesis 6:3. God was distressed at the violence amongst people. This is commented on several times. As a judgment, mankind was to have his life-span reduced to a limit of one hundred and twenty years. (We should not miss a significant implication here: evolutionary progress is based on violence; this is abhorrent to God and so could not have been his creative tool).

Mixed marriage

Genesis 6 opens with a section which has caused much controversy, with probably no satisfactory conclusion. It records the 'sons of God' seeking wives amongst the 'daughters of men'. The clear implications are that this (a) was genetically possible, (b) was not morally permissible, and (c) had significant genetic effects because the descendents gave rise to giants ('*nephilim*'). There have been several explanations of this, but none appears to answer all the problems. To this writer, the natural reading is that the 'sons of God' were the male descendents of Seth and the 'daughters of men' were the women of Cain's family. (I would not be insistent that the terms should be understood specifically in those genders, but, again, it does seem to be the natural interpretation. Also, it is consistent with the tradition of men going to find their wives! Compare Genesis 2:24). We have already noted that Cain's family were separated from God's presence.

Jonathan Stephen, speaking at a conference on Creation[1], has drawn attention to the contrast in the two lines by comparing the references to the two Lamechs. The Cainite Lamech, the first recorded bigamist, prides himself on his brutality (Genesis 4:23-24), whereas the Sethite Lamech contents himself in the peace that God will bring (Genesis 5:29). It has already been noted that the term 'son of God' is synonymous with the 'image of God,' So, the 'sons of God' are the godly line and the 'daughters of men' would appear to indicate an ungodly line. This would be consistent with the practice of Scripture elsewhere. A marriage between the two lines would seem to be in contravention of the Lord's will in separating out Cain from the rest of the family (Genesis 4:10-12).

This event led to God's judgment in the Flood. It is significant that the Bible says 'as it was in the days of Noah' so it will be at the Lord's return (Matthew 24:37-38). The Bible warns plainly against the marriage of Christians and unbelievers (2 Corinthians 6:14) yet we see widespread disobedience to this command today. God's judgment may be imminent because of this.

Since Cain's people had been isolated from Seth's for several generations, there is no reason why genetic traits would not have been developed which would give rise to gigantism. It occurred in post-Flood groups (Numbers 13:32-33; 1 Samuel 17:4; 2 Samuel

21:18-20). Some commentators have regarded this as a reference to great notoriety and wickedness, rather than to great physical stature.

But, this is only one symptom of the godlessness that was growing amongst men. We have already noted God's concern at human violence and so he determines to destroy his creation. (How then does he feel about the violence in the world today — whether abortion, rape, murder, manslaughter, war, muggings, etc.?) As he considered his world, he could only identify one family to spare: that of Noah. He told Noah to build a boat in which he would preserve his family (wife, three sons and their wives) and two of every kind of every living thing. Sufficient food was to be stored also. In particular, Noah was to take on board seven pairs of all 'clean' animals. The reasons for this exception are obvious — some would be used for sacrifice and some for food (Genesis 9:3), so a larger base was necessary to ensure their survival.

The deluge

A week after they entered the boat, the floods lifted them up from the earth. Consider the basic record:

(a) There were forty days and nights of rain during which the 'fountains of the deep' (7:11 — the same word as in 1:2) and the 'windows of heaven' were opened. During this time the water level increased to fifteen cubits above the highest hills; all earth-bound animals and birds died.
(b) For another 110 days, the waters continued to prevail over the whole earth; the 'fountains of the deep' and the 'windows of heaven' were closed — there was no fresh flood water. The boat came to rest, floating above the mountains of Ararat.
(c) The Lord then sent a wind which caused the waters to recede. After nearly three more months, the mountain tops became visible.
(d) Forty days later, we have then the incidents in which Noah released a raven and three doves to see if the ground had dried and the vegetation revived. The birds were released over a period of three weeks.
(e) Nearly two months later, God opened the door and Noah and his family, together with the animals, emerged into a 'new' earth which would be beginning to blossom again.

The extent of the Flood

We must not overlook the clear magnitude of this Flood, otherwise we cannot hope to find correlation between Scripture and observation. The Flood is unambiguously described as destroying *all* life, covering *all* hills. No local flood could achieve that. No local flood could pile up waters to fifteen cubits above the highest hills for most of the year without spreading around the globe! If we do not take the detail of Scripture seriously, we begin to look foolish in our conclusions.

Also, the events of the first forty days are described in dramatic terms. The 'fountains of the deep' burst open to release flood waters. We do not know the full detail here, of course, but the clear implication is that underground caverns of water were released, perhaps following earthquakes. The 'windows of heaven' were opened and allowed torrential rain for forty days. Again, this is an order of magnitude greater than a modern storm, both to last that long and to have that effect. It is consistent with the comment that the waters were gathered above the atmosphere on the second day of creation.

If the causes are so dramatic, then the effects must be so too. Such a quantity of water in such turmoil must have left its mark the world over. It would lead to a redistribution of solid material which would be deposited around the world. Looking at the rock strata, we see two groups of rock layers which are world-wide: the Precambrian and the 'Palaeozoic rocks'. ('Palaeozoic' means 'ancient life'; in these rocks there is a sudden appearance of many kinds of formerly living creatures). There is a discontinuity between these rocks. (Attempts made here to correlate the rock data with this biblical record are tentative. Some Christian geologists are studying this carefully and the comments that follow represent some of the ideas they are advocating).

Geological significance

Joachim Scheven has considered the sequence of geological events following the break-up of the foundations of the deep:
a) the world-wide formation of trough-like depressions (synclines) in the earth's strata and their filling with sediment;

ERA	PERIOD		NOTES	BIBLICAL	
				TIME	REF.
CENOZOIC	QUATERNARY	HOLOCENE PLEISTOCENE	GLACIAL	POST-FLOOD STABILITY	GENESIS 12 - PRESENT
	TERTIARY	PLIOCENE MIOCENE OLIGOCENE EOCENE PALAEOCENE	SANDS & CLAY		
MESOZOIC	CRETACEOUS		CHALK CLAY	POST-FLOOD INSTABILITY	GENESIS 10 - 11
	JURASSIC		CLAY		
	TRIASSIC		SAND & MARL		
PALAEOZOIC	UPPER	PERMIAN	LIMESTONE & MARL	FLOOD LAYERS	GENESIS 7 - 9
		CARBONIFEROUS	COAL MEASURES		
		DEVONIAN	SANDSTONE & LIMESTONE		
		SILURIAN	LIMESTONE & SHALES		
	LOWER	ORDOVICIAN	SHALES & VOLCANICS		
		CAMBRIAN	SLATES & SANDSTONES		
PRECAMBRIAN		PROTEROZOIC		CREATION & PRE-FLOOD STABILITY	GENESIS 2 -6 GENESIS 1:3 - 31
		ARCHAEOZOIC	METAMORPHIC AND IGNEOUS		GENESIS 1:2: JOB 38:6 - 9
		AZOIC			GENESIS 1:1

Figure 13: A creationist view of the geological strata

b) the formation and decanting of temporary epicontinental seas (that is, seas covering the land mass) and the emergence of surfaces with the characteristics of deserts;

c) the violent fracturing, movement and distending of the earth's crust.

He proposes that these incidents took place respectively

a) in the Flood year,

b) from the Flood year to the time of Peleg and

c) then in the following couple of centuries up to the beginning of the Ice Age.

The observed geological data also show that there is a one-way development of geological history; there are successive stages through which the earth has only passed once. This is in accord with biblical history too.

There is no parallel between the geological column (see below) and the normal, non-catastrophic processes of today. Further, fossiliferous rocks are not observed to be forming around us now.

The *geological column* is a theoretical reconstruction of the earth's geological history (see figure 13). It is constructed by combining all the different rock layers observed around the world in a logical sequence and of thicknesses corresponding to the largest deposit in each case. It should be noted that this theoretical sequence of deposition is not found in reality anywhere in the world. The consequent assumption is that this sequence of rocks was steadily deposited over large periods of time.

Fossils

One significant difference between the Precambrian and the Palaeozoic rocks is the very small number of fossils in the Precambrian rocks. It is suggested here that these rocks were laid following the Creation week (see chapter 4) with perhaps some further depositions or changes from the time of the Fall to the Flood. The Palaeozoic rocks are fossilized and, we believe, were deposited in the Flood.

The creationist model will predict that complex creatures (for example, fish, amphibia, etc) will appear in the rocks complete and without simpler precedents. This is what has been observed, even in the Precambrian sediments.

On this creationist model, the rocks were laid over a relatively short period of time, in contrast to the popular views. So, the fossil record is a snap-shot of the earth at the time and is not a reflection of biological development over large periods of time. The species trapped in the rocks show stasis (periods of uninterrupted change) and an absence of intermediate kinds.

Any morphological changes seen in the fossils will be observed in organisms that have short generation time — that is, a generation time shorter than the time represented by the series of catastrophes. Local catastrophes will reflect the local conditions and so the biogeographic distribution of organisms and their generation times: animals with larger generation times will not be sufficiently numerous to appear until later depositions. Even then, such depositions will not necessarily mark complete extinctions — except possibly in those localities. From this we can deduce that the Palaeozoic layers are likely to have been formed in the Flood year (this chapter) and the Cenozoic strata after it (chapter 8), the term Cenozoic indicating the most recent rocks.

Environmental conditions can affect the rate of regeneration too. For example, a build-up of atmospheric carbon dioxide in the oceans would favour the rapid formation of shelled creatures. An abnormally high population would result. This could lead to 'tragedy' if there were insufficient food for these creatures. Catastrophic deposition would lead to massive chalk deposits, for example.

Stratification

There is stratification within the Flood-deposited (Palaeozoic) layers, which has been shown to be possible even in tumultuous processes, not only in laboratory experiments but it has also been observed in natural processes. An example of this was observed in the 1980 eruption of Mount St Helens in Washington, USA. In this, the eruption produced a lava flow. When the solidified rock was studied, it was found that the rock was clearly and linearly stratified, in spite of the speed and turbulence of the flow. For example, the pyroclastic flow (see the glossary) produced a 25 foot thick deposit in one day and this consists of many laminae (very thin layers) and beds. A similar result was observed in the Bijou Creek flood in Colorado during 1965. There were forty-eight hours of rain and up to twelve feet of sediment were deposited. When the deposits were studied, it was found that over 90% of the sediment was stratified. In fact, stratification of the type observed does not occur in still water conditions.

The processes of stratification in turbulent flood flow have been studied in the laboratory by Guy Berthault. It has traditionally been assumed that the continuous linear stratification in the rocks indicates that they were deposited in periods of geological quietness. The above observations from nature and the work of Berthault have shown that these assumptions are incorrect. These experiments have shown that, during the turbulent flow, the particles are sorted by such physical factors as size and laid down simultaneously. The deposition is in the direction of flow, so that, effectively, these deposits are laid simultaneously. Consequently, sedimentary deposits along a coast-line are not older at the bottom (as normally assumed) but at the beginning of the direction of flow. As Professor Derek Ager, a geologist who opposes any concept of creation, has said, sedimentation is lateral not vertical.

The fossil content of the Palaeozoic rocks is stunning. It has been called the Cambrian explosion (the Cambrian stratum being the lowest of the Palaeozoic rocks). Suddenly, in terms of the rock distribution, a wide range of fossils is found. Almost all the major phyla (see the glossary) are represented, including the simpler vertebrates occurring in later strata. Many of the animals and plants would have been trapped in the sediment and fossilized. Others would have been destroyed without trace. (Normal processes of death lead to decay and the scattering of the bones). Probably much of the living order was destroyed even in the first few days of the Flood. The Flood had a dramatic effect — certainly in forty days, all life was destroyed.

It is usually assumed that the rocks are full of fossils of all types. In fact, 95% of the fossil record is made up of shallow marine organisms (for example, trilobites, corals and fish). 95% of the rest consists of algae and plant fossils. The vertebrates make up 0.25% and only 1% *of these* involve fossils of more than one bone.

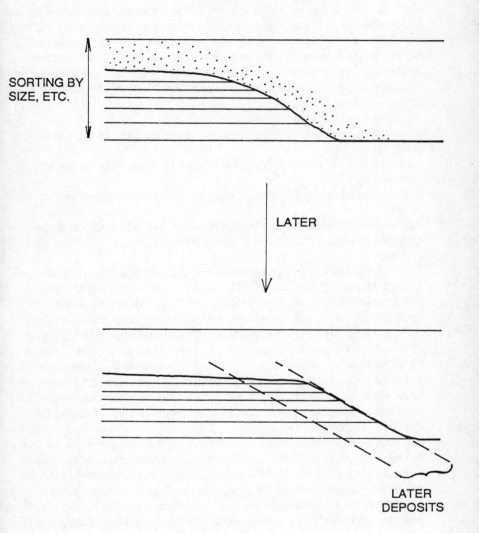

Figure 14: Sedimentation and stratification.

Destruction of the vertebrates

Why should there be so few vertebrate fossils and then only in later deposits? The Flood would result in the rapid burial of the relatively immobile shallow marine organisms. With the beginning of the Flood, most land-based animals and humans would have moved to higher ground. What would happen to their bodies? A number of possible processes would result in the loss of their remains. Andrew Snelling, a mining consultant, has identified some of these:

decomposition of floating bodies;
destruction of the bodies by agitation and abrasion in the Flood waters;
vulnerability of floating bodies as food to birds and to marine carnivores;
destruction of deposited material through oxidation by permeating water;
destruction of fossilized material when original sediments undergo change (*metamorphism*) due to heat and pressure.

In addition, God said that he would destroy mankind from the face of the earth (Genesis 6:7). The word *destroy* is frequently used in Scripture to indicate complete obliteration. So, it would not be suprising if the Flood deposits contained no human remains.

Undoubtedly the single land mass would have begun to break up at this time. During the subsequent five months, there would have been continuing movement of the earth as it settled from the geological upheaval, just as modern earthquakes continue for some time with after effects. More depositions, upheavals, *etc.* would occur. It would seem likely that these changes are demonstrated in the early Palaeozoic rocks.

The next three months are marked by receding waters and strong winds that gradually dry the land. Mountain tops appeared as land movements caused them to rise. During this period, the waters would come and go from the land, leaving deposits. These effects would be more localized than the earlier ones and may be represented in the upper Palaeozoic strata. The land would then have dried out as the waters left it to return to the seas; new boundaries would have been established, closing the Palaeozoic era.

As they left the boat, Noah and his family sacrificed in thanksgiving to God. The new world order was marked by a new covenant. God promised seasons of seedtime and harvest (Genesis 8:22). It is possible that the pre-Flood earth had a uniform, non-seasonal climate but, in any case, God promised that the new world would be fruitful to feed mankind. (Certainly geological evidence seems to emphasize that the early earth had a uniform tropical climate). God also permitted the people to eat meat in the future (Genesis 9:3).

The world had been punished because of its violence. God reemphasized this by reiterating the command against murder (Genesis 9:6). The ultimate reason for this, we are told, is that mankind is made in God's image.

Finally, God pointed Noah to the rainbow which is to serve as a reminder to him that God will not again destroy the earth in this way. Judgment has been executed. The new world was to be repopulated through Noah's family and the animals that had been packed into the boat.

The expression used in Genesis 6-10 for the Flood (and in the New Testament reference to the same event) is unique. It refers to a deluge, to a cataclysmic event. It is not a natural or common experience. It was divinely ordered, done in judgment and for salvation (of Noah, his family and descendants).

This experience was to serve as a reminder to people of all generations that God will judge this world for its sin. It is only in his mercy that we are allowed to continue in this way. As in the days of Noah, so it will be when the King of kings returns (Matthew 24:36-39; 2 Peter 3:6-7).

Reference

1. Jonathan Stephen, 'A Biblical Look at Early Civilisation,' Origins, 1993, 5(14), 18-22.

8.
After the flood

When the flood waters receded, the earth quickly blossomed again with plant life. This is clear from the leaf brought to Noah by the dove and from natural observation. A volcanic island, Surtsey, was produced off Iceland in 1963-7. One of the remarkable features was how quickly plant life appeared on this island. This was less likely than after the Flood, because Surtsey was igneous rock and not flood sediment. Similarly, after the Mount St Helens eruption of 1980, a large variety of life became established rapidly. (We are assuming that only 'natural' processes were involved and not miraculous ones in the post-Flood recovery).

It should be obvious that there would be substantial after-effects from such a global disturbance. This would probably correspond to time known as the Mesozoic ('middle life') period. (Indeed, one may argue that, based on biblical chronology, we are still experiencing some of these disturbing geological effects). As the earth stabilized, it moved into the Cenozoic period ('recent life'). So, we are proposing, that the Palaeozoic rocks correspond to the Flood year, the Mesozoic rocks to the years immediately following the Flood; the Cenozoic rocks are those of the next few centuries. See figure 13 for a summary of these times.

Rapid processes

As the massive flood waters drained from the land, they would have eroded into the freshly deposited strata. The rapid effects of such processes are again demonstrated at Mount St Helens. This volcano deposited a plain of pumice which was eroded in one day by a mud flow to give a miniature version of the 'Grand Canyon' (approximately one-fortieth scale).

Clearly, such processes do not need millions of years. The fact that erosion is completed over a much shorter period of time is also demonstrated by observing the rock strata around the world. It is noticeable that the strata are virtually always linear and parallel without any significant erosion. Yet, erosion processes such as that just described can be rapid. In fact, erosion can be observed at the vertical edges of rocks whereas it is not observed in the horizontal planes in some sites.

There are stages in the deposition of rocks where it is clear that there are discontinuities in the process. A series of strata are laid down and then there is a time gap before the subsequent layers are deposited. Such boundaries occur, for example, between the Permian and Triassic layers. But even here the time gap is relatively short. The erosion is not what one would expect from exposure over millions of years (or, indeed, thousands).

When the top of a particular layer of sedimentary rock was the top of the sea bed or land (that is, before the next rock layers were deposited), it would be very vulnerable to damage. For example, even in a few hours it will be subject to the scouring effects of the sea — it could not survive even centuries unscathed. Sea bed layers would also be exposed to the effects of animals (shrimps, worms, crabs, *etc.*) which would dig into it. Land surfaces would be exposed to more atmospheric processes, as well as the effects of animals. One remarkable feature of recent volcanic processes (for example, at Surtsey and at Mount St. Helens) has been the rapid process of rehabitation by animals and the growth of plants on the surface of the newly deposited rocks. We can reasonably expect, therefore, much much more significant disturbances at the discontinuities if there are large time gaps.

Similarly, the processes of folding so often observed in mountainous areas are more easily explained on the Flood model than on the long age model, because the rocks would be more pliable. The hard rocks would be brittle and so would fracture.

Another process that is often thought to take millions of years is the formation of peat and coal. Again we can turn to Mount St Helens. The effect of the eruption was to cause a massive tidal wave in Spirit Lake. This swept a million trees from the hillside. The trees

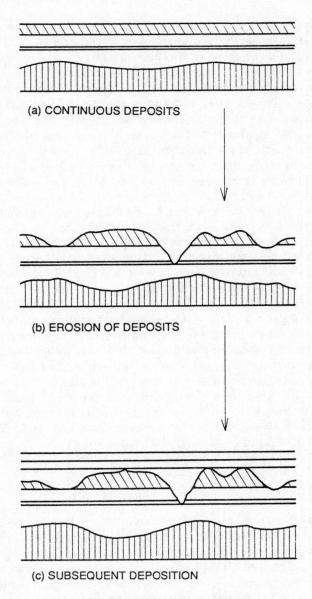

(a) CONTINUOUS DEPOSITS

(b) EROSION OF DEPOSITS

(c) SUBSEQUENT DEPOSITION

Figure 15: Predicted erosion pattern.
The accepted geological timescale should give erosion — deposition patterns as in
(c). In fact, (a) is the common observation or (b), if erosion has occurred.

were ripped from their roots and stripped of the bark and branches. The trees floated in the lake and the bark and branches settled on the bottom. Within three years, this base had turned to peat.

It is often thought that formations such as chalk cliffs must have taken millions of years to form by comparing the number of shell creatures in the sea today with those required to form such cliffs. There is some false reasoning here. Aside from the fact that there is evidence that such layers had to form fast, it assumes that the present population of the sea is the determining factor. After the Flood, the concentration of nutrients in the water would probably have been high. This would have generated rapid growth in population which could then have been extinguished suddenly. Obviously, too, the creatures need not have all been local but could have accumulated in that region by water flows. It is quite probable that the carbonate concentration was also high at this time and this too would have encouraged rapid growth. Scheven has studied the oyster-reef in Germany and noted that the rate of growth of the chalk was probably many times greater than that normally assumed. Also, the creatures did not mature: they were only 10 mm in size rather than the normal 5 cm. So, the period of growth was short but permitted rapid growth. The death of these organisms was catastrophic. It appears that they lived, spawned and died in abnormal conditions within days rather than millennia. It is reminiscent of badly disturbed ecosystems today resulting in population explosions ('blooms').

A well-known phenomenon is the presence of polystrate trees. The trees have been vertically fossilized across several layers of strata. These strata could not have taken millions of years to deposit or else the exposed parts would have rotted away.

Fossils

The very existence of fossils indicates that the rocks must be laid in a short period of time. If the creatures which became fossilised lay on the surface awaiting a complete covering, they will decay or be eaten by predators. Consider the data usually used by those who consider that natural, non-catastrophic events cause sedimentation. Their figures for the rate of formation of the geological column is of the order of 0.02 mm a year. That is less deposition than will settle as dust in your bedroom! It is about the thickness of a hair and finer

Figure 16: A polystrate tree.

than a grain of sand. So, to bury a shrimp in order to fossilize it, we would need tens of thousands of years! What of our dinosaur or the polystrate tree? The evidence again favours rapid burial. Since we have shown that the time between layers was too short for erosion, the whole column must have been laid very rapidly.

The new post-Flood order would continue to involve the effects of sin at the Fall: death and sickness. In addition, the length of life was shortened, as promised before the Flood. Another result of sin, and a consequence of the Flood, was the extinction of species from time to time. As the geological effects occurred and climatic changes too, some animals which found an initial ecological niche were destroyed. This is a continuing reminder to us — as we can still observe it — of the effects of sin. The whole of nature groans awaiting the final redemption (Romans 8:22).

Fossil distribution

There is an arrangement of fossils between the strata which led many to think it would provide evidence for no-God processes of development. Few leading evolutionists would wish to base their confidence now on the rock and fossil record because it is not conclusive.

The repopulation of the world after the Flood would have taken different lengths of time for different species. The period would be determined by a number of factors: regeneration times, availability of food, the climate, *etc.* There would be a period of rapid growth from the initial population, then some fluctuation until a period of stability was attained. Sedimentation would reflect the population at that time and locality. The relative populations would be very variable in the years following the Flood until an equilibrium was reached.

The presence of the fossils does not, of course, represent the time of origin or extinction. Frequently it is assumed that the fossils occur in isolated layers during which time they were eliminated. In fact, a large proportion of the fossilized animals have survived unchanged to the present day. Around 90% of the present living families of terrestrial vertebrates (excluding birds) are found in the fossil record. So, it is no problem to find fossilized creatures still 'alive and well'. For example, a fish called the coelacanth appears in the Palaeozoic and Mesozoic rocks (said to have been laid down up to about 100 million years ago), but it was found alive in 1938 in the Indian Ocean off South Africa. Rather than being an intermediate form which struggled to crawl on the land, it is perfectly designed for multi-directional movement. Also, we are not surprised to find that the creature is unchanged over the period of time between fossilization and the present. An evolutionary scenario would require significant mutational changes to have occurred, yet fossilized creatures and their modern counterparts are usually identical.

Joachim Scheven has collected much evidence in his museum (in Germany) demonstrating the continuity between fossilized creatures and plants and the modern ones. In particular, he has studied many creatures trapped in amber. These are supposedly from forty to over a hundred million years old (depending on the location of the amber). The creatures are often no different from those observed today. Typical examples of these include the cockroach, bees, ants, the fruit fly, a snail and a frog.

Very recently, teams of researchers have been analysing the DNA in some of these insects and have noted that, even at this level, there is little significant difference between the fossilized and modern forms.

Dinosaurs

One of the so-called pre-historic creatures that fascinates man is the dinosaur, though there are many identified types of dinosaur. They demonstrate a number of useful points. First of all, we find that they occur in the Triassic, Jurassic and Cretaceous periods and suddenly disappear from the geological record. But, is it a time of *extinction* of the creature or just an extermination of large numbers in those localities? In other words, do the fossil deposits of an animal represent its demise from the earth or could it still occur in the world today? Further, if our reading of Scripture is correct, these geological deposits did not pre-date man, but occurred in his lifetime. So, were dinosaurs and man contemporary?

To answer these questions, which can obviously be extended to other fossilized animals and plants, we need to remember that the word *dinosaur* (meaning 'terrible lizard') is a modern word. So, we will not find it used in ancient literature such as the Bible. Do we

find, though, descriptions (in words or art) that are consistent with
the dinosaur? For example, Job 40 refers to the *behemoth*. This has
been described as an elephant or even a rhinoceros, yet the description fits a dinosaur far better. The passage speaks of the creature
having a tail like a cedar tree. That is far more like the dinosaur, such
as the *brachiosaurus*, than an elephant or rhinoceros. Pictures have
also been found in various parts of the world (e.g. in cave drawings)
which resemble them.

Also, Job 41 speaks of the *leviathan*, which could be a sea-going
dinosaur, rather than the crocodile as often thought (cf. Isaiah 27:1).
Again we read of the leviathan frolicking in the sea (Psalm 104:26)
which is not a particularly realistic description of a crocodile.
Japanese fishermen in 1977 caught and photographed a dead
creature identified as a *pleisosaur*. The modern Komodo Dragon
(*Varanus komodiensis*) is a creature similar to the dinosaur: it is up
to ten feet long and 300 lb in weight and that is still around. In recent
years, dinosaur bones have been found mixed with those of animals
similar to the modern horse, cow and sheep.

The Ice Age

Recent work by Michael Oard indicates that the Ice Age (of the so-
called Pleistocene period) can be readily explained on the biblical
model. The volcanic activity that would have accompanied the
Flood would have caused great amounts of dust to be thrown into the
atmosphere. This would have caused significant drops in the
summer temperatures. In addition, the opening of the 'fountains of
the deep' would have released hot water which would have raised
the ocean temperatures. This, aided by the winds, would have
produced greater evaporation and further cooling. The effect would
be the formation of glaciers which would not have melted in the
summers.[1]

Babel

Genesis 11 refers to some significant events. One is the dispersion
of the people at Babel. Because of man's pride, seeking to elevate
himself in the place of God (the same sin as Lucifer! Isaiah
14:12-15), God confused his language so that he had to split into
social groups that could understand one another. This was the

beginning of the nations. There is an interesting implication here. It is easy to assume, on a creationist model, that all languages came from a common source and so seek to trace the history of their natural development. This passage is a warning that research into a common language source *may* not be successful. There is no direct evidence from a study of linguistics that modern languages derive naturally from a universal proto-language.

There is an interesting archaeological find housed in the British Museum. It is from the Mesopotamian region and is an engraved cylinder commemorating the rebuilding of a *ziggurat* to the goddess Ishtar and it is noted that this event (conventionally dated to about 1850 BC) is 'seven generations after the dynasty of Akkad'. One cannot be too certain here, but it is interesting that this would be consistent with the time of the attempts at Babel (based on the Old Testament genealogies, *etc.*).

It is also interesting to note that we find myths around the world which all reflect (albeit in a distorted form) the record of a common origin and universal flood. This commonality disappears after the Babel event — as one would expect from the biblical record: after this time the various peoples of the world ceased to have any common history.

We are also told about Peleg, so-called because in his time the earth was divided. This could refer to the dispersal of the people following the confusion of the languages at Babel. Probably though, in view of the use of the word 'earth,' it refers to the break-up of the land mass, so corresponding to the Cretaceous period of geology. Obviously this requires a short fracture time for the land mass and, perhaps, a slower time of drift until the final disruption of the land mass into the present day continents. A tensile fracture in igneous rock, which is the main base of the earth, occurs at nearly 2 km per second. At this rate, the initial land mass could be broken up in eight hours. This would require a different mechanism to that usually proposed for the continental break-up, but could be consistent with the model described.

Early man and culture

The other point of significance here is the development of culture.

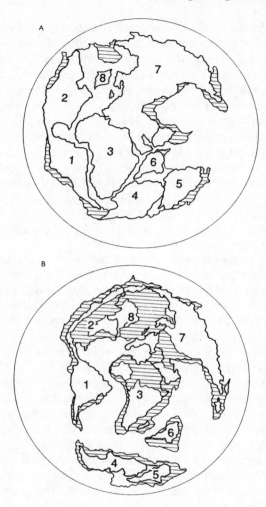

Figure 17: Break-up of the land mass.
The land mass with outline of modern continents (dark lines) and epicontinental seas (shaded areas).
    A. The earth at the palaeozoic mesozoic interface.
    B. The earth at the upper cretaceous period.

Key:	1. South America	2. North America	3. Africa
	4. Antarctica	5. Australasia	6. India
	7. Eurasia	8. Greenland	

The biblical model describes human beings as intelligent, not developing intelligence but knowledge. It is not surprising, therefore, to see the record describing rapid developments in agriculture (Genesis 4:20), metallurgy (Genesis 4:22), the arts (Genesis 4:21), *etc.* These passages refer to developments before the Flood. They would probably have been rapid after the Flood with Noah's knowledge of these earlier skills. In fact, the biblical model would predict degradation in culture because of sin from a high level (relative to animals) rather than a development from the animal culture because of evolution. This is in keeping with the comments we have made on man in the image of God. Interpretations of early man (e.g. Stone Age Man, Neanderthal, *etc.*) must be understood in this light too.[4] This is in contrast the view developed from an evolutionary explanation which sees our remote ancestors as unsophisticated primitives only a step removed from the apes.

The biblical model of mankind is significantly different from the humanistic one. According to the Bible, people have always been intelligent (having been created in God's image), but were almost completely destroyed in the Flood. Those who survived (Noah and his family) retained a knowledge of technology *etc.* but lost the means for its immediate implementation. They continued as a group in the Mesopotamian region until they were eventually dispersed following the Babel incident.

Palaeolithic Man ('Old Stone Age') of archaeology is unmistakably human, living in caves and hunting for food. He was a wanderer, moving to locate new food sources. He produced very efficient flint tools, used harpoons (similar to the modern Eskimo), made cave paintings, developed musical instruments and believed in an after-life. He probably included the 'Neanderthal' and 'Cromagnon' men of archaeology. Diseases such as arthritis and rickets have been detected in his remains and this will explain many of the characteristic features of Neanderthal Man. A discovery of remains in Yugoslavia provides evidence of nursing care leading to healing. It is clear that Neanderthals did not precede modern man because findings in Israel show that modern humans predated Neanderthals (who used tools of similar quality) by many years. Palaeolithic Man probably fits into the period of climatic instability following the Flood (Genesis 9:19 and 10:32).

He was succeeded by Neolithic Man ('New Stone Age') who controlled his environment and became a farmer. He is known for his production of axes, for his mining and the construction of megalithic structures. Though there is evidence of a semi-nomadic existence, it is also clear that he settled in some areas. The distribution of the stone tools showed that there was a mobility and trade between such communities. The precision of the megaliths shows an outstanding mathematical ability and engineering skills. He had a complex social structure involving designers, architects, surveyors, miners, builders, *etc*. Evidence has also been found of glue and string, the ability to make shoes and clothes, the manufacture of bows, arrows and spears and of the construction of sculptures. These observations are consistent with the scattering after the time of Peleg (Genesis 10:25).

Biogeography

These facts are also consistent with the biogeographical distribution of species. When the land mass was a whole and the repopulation was rapid, all kinds of creatures - man, animals, insects, *etc.* - would have spread. The break up of the land mass would have then isolated groups which would undergo differentiation due to the different environments (e.g. the ice covering). Biogeographical distribution would also be affected by anthropogenic factors (that is, selectivity by man).

As we have seen, there is much built-in genetic information. Light-coloured animals in a dark environment would be vulnerable and liable to extinction. The well-known effect of the peppered moth in England illustrates this. The dark-coloured species dominated during the dirty climate of the post-Industrial Revolution period. The effects of the Clean Air Act have allowed the light coloured one to recover before its complete extinction.

Changes occurred following the Flood in the earth's geology, in man's dispersion, *etc.* Some of these are still being observed today. The Bible indicates these observations both explicitly and implicitly.

References

1. M J Oard, 'An Ice Age caused by the Genesis Flood,' Institute of Creation Research, 1990.

2. D Tyler, 'A New Vista on the New Stone Age,' Origins, 1989, 2(6), 8-12; *ibid*, 'Ancient Civilisations' in 'Focus on Creation,' Rainbow Press, 1978.

9.
The implications of creation

As we have moved through these early chapters of Genesis, we have seen that the observable data is consistent with the record. We have also seen something of the implications of various statements, especially those concerned with the nature of man.

Ultimately, though, we can never prove the truth of the record. It is a unique and, therefore, unrepeatable event. We cannot go back in time and observe it happening. We believe in creation because we believe the Bible to be God's infallible Word. It is an act of faith (Hebrew 11:3), but it is not 'blind faith'. We know 'whom we have believed' (2 Timothy 1:12). He has proved himself trustworthy in all matters, so we have no reason to doubt his testimony.

That creation is by his word means that it is by his power and intelligence. The living system is full of purpose and in-built meaning. It is not haphazard or by chance. To say that creation is 'at his word' also means that he is transcendent. This undermines such movements as the 'New Age', which believes that God is identical with his universe. All creation is subject to him. It must obey his word and do his will. It came into being at his command. It will be dissolved at his command (2 Peter 3). The world and its order had a miraculous origin and will have a miraculous destiny.

The creation was spoiled by man's willing sin. Even at that time, when God must have been very angry, we see his mercy. He promises redemption. The seed of the woman would be the Saviour of mankind. The God who created man was, through Man, to bring his salvation. If he were not able to create man, he would not be able to bring about the miraculous conception of the Lord Jesus.

The Bible makes it plain that death is the result of sin (Romans 5:12). Christ died for our sins. Paul says that we obtain 'salvation through our Lord Jesus Christ, who died for us' (1 Thessalonians 5:9-10). As by one man, Adam, came death, so by the last Adam will come the resurrection of the dead (Romans 5:14-15). He who created the heavens and the earth will create a new heavens and earth (Isaiah 65:17; 66:22; 2 Peter 3:13; Revelations 21:1). The same actions are described.

The Scriptures indicate that the world was created by God for man's pleasure and provision. It is to be enjoyed with gratitude (Psalm 104; 1 Timothy 4:1-5). It is to be used and cared for, but not exploited. Man is a steward who is accountable to his Maker.

There is a sharp difference in our interpretation of man's history and that of the non-Christian. The interpretations that ignore God and his plans, see man as developing from a primitive form with little intelligence and gradually becoming culturally more sophisticated. The Bible presents him as a complete and perfect creation from the outset with intelligence and extensive faculties. He is made in the image of his Creator. Consequently, there is a difference in attitude to man. To the Christian, he is special and matters as an individual.

That a belief in creation by God makes a difference from a belief in a no-God process is clearly apparent. Paul made this plain in his preaching (Acts 14:15-17; 17:22-31). Creation reminds us that we are accountable to God. We are persuaded that human life is precious and not to be disposed of as we will. It is plain that man is precious to God (John 3:16) and we must value his soul highly and bring him news of the Creator, the Saviour of mankind.

Creation and God's promises

The bottom line is the reliability of God's Word. Our belief in creation is based on his testimony. Is it trustworthy? If we cannot believe him in Genesis 1 and 2, why should we believe him in Genesis 3:15? If he did not create the world as recorded, the decalogue has no validity because Exodus 20:8-11 is meaningless and deceptive. Morality will be undermined because in this primary statement, the decalogue, he would be shown to be a liar. (It is significant that there is no decalogue for the animal kingdom, emphasising the distance between us). If John 1:3 is not true, then how can we believe in John 1:12? If Hebrews 11:3 is not true, what hope do we have of an eternal rest (Hebrews 4:3-5)?

The Scriptures also teach that God is sovereign in creation. Is the world by no-God chance or by God's control? Is it 'very good' (Genesis 1:31) or is it the result of a battle by 'nature red in tooth and claw'? Creation demonstrates that man is answerable to God. The creature does not challenge the Creator (Job 40:3-5).

To speak of creation is to state that God is in control. God's plan is being worked out. History is his story. God cannot be frustrated in his purposes.

Ethics and doctrine

The biblical account demonstrates that sin brings death and man is responsible. The only explanation of evil is in the Bible. Evil brings death and the effect of it is demonstrated in the decreasing age span of mankind, which again has no 'natural' explanation. Christ's death was for our sins. There would be no point in his death if death has no connection with sin. His resurrection, the conquest of death, was physical. It is not solely in the spiritual realm; the battle with sin has a physical consequence too (1 Corinthians 15:21-22). If sin is a meaningless concept, so is redemption. Mankind cannot be redeemed for something that has no penalty or guilt. People cannot be blamed for sin if it is a mere side-effect of the evolutionary process.

A belief in creation has an effect on the 'work ethic'. A process based on struggle for survival as the only motivation does not have an ethic for work. For the creationist, we see that work was an opportunity, a responsibility, given at the time of creation. Man must work to be fulfilled. We must work to meet the divine mandate. God himself is presented as a worker. We recognize that work, like all else, has been corrupted by the Fall (Genesis 3:19). The doctrine of creation also emphasizes the need for one day of rest in each week. Society must, therefore, not just expect a person to work, but also accept that it has a responsibility to assist him in that endeavour. Of course, there is more to the concept of work than paid labour. Many a woman works in the home unpaid!

The Christian view of marriage is linked to creation (Matthew 19:4-8; 1 Corinthians 11:8). It is significant that the rejection of the doctrine of creation has been accompanied (inside the church as well as outside) by unparalleled levels of marriage breakdown. Again, we have a responsibility to preserve the family. We have already seen that the human family is unique in its nature over against the families observed in the rest of the natural order. It was deliberately formed at creation and society and the church must do all they can to protect this divine institution. Too often, even in evangelical circles, the family becomes subservient to work in the church or employment. But it is not to be. We are not fulfilling the divine concern if we do not protect and encourage the family unit (see, for example, 1 Timothy 4:3).

The new creation is a parallel to the original. Is the new creation evolutionary too? That is how many non-Christian religions see religious experience. Rather, God is making us into the 'image of his Son' (Romans 8:29). He re-creates us. The wording is a deliberate link to the Genesis account. Biblical creation is a philosophy of hope and not despair.

Professor Edgar Andrews[1] has shown how closely the scriptures tie in the doctrines of Christ as Creator and Saviour. Typical passages that can be studied are John 1, Colossians 1 and Hebrews 1. Other passages with the same theme are Ephesians 1:4-5 and 1 Timothy 1:8-9. The Bible knows of no separation between these two doctrines.

To reject one is to reject the other. So, the biblical understanding of creation is tied closely to the doctrines of the church, which have been developed from scripture. We have seen how much of biblical theology is undermined by evolutionary thinking. We believe that the biblical doctrine of creation is not only scientifically consistent but is scripturally necessary and is a consistent part of the whole body of theology. Those who would try to marry the no-God philosophy with the biblical one have serious problems. Not only do they have to face the scientific problems, but they have serious theological problems. They need to write a whole new body of theology.

Peter, in his second letter (third chapter), predicts the current skepticism concerning the early chapters of the scriptures. He tells of people who would scoff at the return of Christ. They will say, 'Things are just as they have always been.' This is what we hear today. But, says Peter, it escapes their notice that God has intervened in the past:

a) by God's word, the Earth was formed and then destroyed in the Flood, and
b) by his word, the Earth today is being reserved for the final judgment.

Peter tells us that the Lord is patient, not influenced by the passage of time (for he is eternal), giving time for people to repent. BUT, suddenly his judgment WILL come and he will create a new heaven and earth. So, says Peter, we must be diligent in practice and faithful to the scriptures.

We have not only the testimony of God himself, but he has left the evidence for those who will recognize it. Paul tells us that 'since the creation of the world his invisible attributes ... have been clearly seen, being understood through what has been made, so that they are without excuse.' (Romans 1:20).

The Christian looks on the world and the seas, beyond the ravages of sin, and exclaims,

'Then sings my soul, my Saviour God, to thee,
How great thou art! How great thou art.'

Reference

1. Edgar H. Andrews, Origins, 1993, 6 (15),2-5.

Appendix A
The cell and its constituents

People, animals and plants are made up of a combination of many units called cells. They are three-dimensional and figure 18 shows a cross-section of a generalised animal cell.

There are essentially two regions to the cell, each enclosed by a membrane: the nucleus and the cytoplasm. The nucleus controls cell action, the cytoplasm being the region in which the processes themselves take place. It can be likened to a chemical industrial plant (and a very complex one at that!).

The nucleus is the 'computerized control centre' of the cell in that analogy.

The cytoplasm is the larger part of the chemical factory. There are two main centres in this: the mitochondria (which are the 'power house'), the ribosomes — which are sited on the endoplasmic reticulum — (and these are the protein 'factories'). The detailed structures of all these parts are complex and an interesting study in design in themselves!

The raw materials of the cell are:

carbohydrates (sugars and starches) which are important for energy production;

glycerides (fats and oils) which are also important for energy production;

proteins (made by linking amino acid units), which are important in structural components of many tissues and are the active part of enzymes, some hormones, blood proteins, *etc.*;

nucleic acids - these combine (using phosphate-sugar links) to give the 'computer tapes' (the DNA) and 'messengers' (RNA).

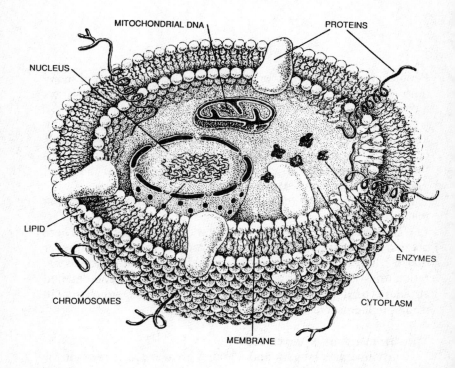

Figure 18: Cross-section of a typical cell.

Appendix B
Dating by radioactivity

In spite of the geological evidence adduced for rapid deposition of the rocks, the question is often raised concerning the use of radioactivity for measuring age. Surely, the argument goes, these 'clocks' show that the world *is* very old? Let us look at some of the principles and their implications.

The idea is very simple and can be related to a burning candle. Imagine entering a room in which a candle is burning. Can you determine when it was lit? We can measure the rate at which it burns away and, assuming it burnt at the same rate before you entered the room, you could estimate how long it had been burning. BUT, this is only possible if the following conditions are true:

a) you knew how long the candle was when it was lit, and

b) you know that the rate of combustion was constant. Alternatively,

c) you could weigh all the smoke and gas produced in burning and so calculate the original length.

The problems are that we do not know the original length of the candle, the rate of combustion can vary (for example, in a draft) and we would have to be sure that no smoke or gas escaped!

This situation is analogous to that in radiometric dating.

Some chemical elements emit radiation. Some elements exist in several forms or weights and have different 'activities' (rates of decay). These are quoted as *halflives*. For example, for carbon there are a number of forms (*isotopes*):

Isotope	Half-life
carbon-11	20.5 minutes
carbon-12	completely stable
carbon-14	5730 years

The half-life is the time taken for the element to decay into half the amount (see figure 19). Carbon-14 takes nearly six thousand years to decay into half its original amount. The equivalent of the candle's smoke, in the case of carbon-14, is nitrogen-14 (which is a natural component of the earth's atmosphere).

The difference from a candle is that the half-life does not depend on the initial amount. The half-life is the same whether we start with 10 grams, 10 kilograms or 10 milligrams.

It is important to note that the half-lives of significance to our topic fall into two groups as shown in the following examples:

Isotopes	Half-lives
1) carbon-14	5 730 years
2) potassium-40	1 300 000 000 years
uranium-238	4 510 000 000 years
rubidium-80	48 800 000 000 years

The first category consists of carbon-14 only and its half-life is a few thousand years. The others are of the order of thousands of millions of years. Further, the carbon-14 occurs in living things (plants, animals) whereas the others only occur in non-living rock material.

One other general point is worthy of note. As a general rule, the amount of radiation is negligible after a period about ten times as long as the half-life. So, for example, after 60 000 years, the amount of carbon-14 left is negligible.

With these facts, let us consider some of the common radiometric techniques.

Carbon-14 dating

All living things contain carbon. Carbon (as in plants) contains two isotopes in nature: carbon-12 and carbon-14. This, in turn, is taken up from the atmosphere and is also eaten by animals. So, there is a

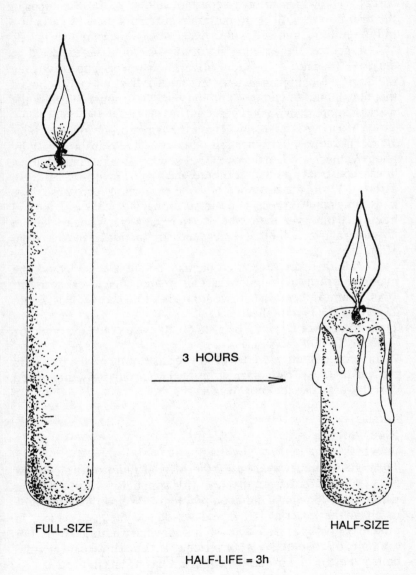

FULL-SIZE   HALF-SIZE

HALF-LIFE = 3h

Figure 19: Half-life of a candle.

carbon cycle which ensures a constant amount of these isotopes in the natural order. (The proportion is tiny, less than 10 parts in a million million, but well within experimental measurement).

Of course, the amount of carbon-14 would be expected to decrease (because it is radioactive). However, due to cosmic radiation, it is being regenerated (figure 20). It is generally believed that the amount of carbon-14 is constant. This must be true if the world is more than 60 000 years old.

When a tree is alive, it will have the same proportion of carbon-14 as the atmosphere, because it is constantly absorbing it by photosynthesis. When the tree is cut down (to make a boat, build a house, construct a piece of furniture, etc.), it no longer absorbs fresh carbon-14 from the atmosphere, so the proportion decreases. If we know how much is present now in our archaeological specimen and how much there was there when the tree was alive, we can calculate how long ago it died. (This corresponds to situations *a* and *b* on page 107).

While there are several problems inherent in this method, the main one is in the assumption that there is a constant level of carbon-14 in the atmosphere. In fact, we are at least 15% short of that (figure 21). This has two implications:
1) the living world cannot be even 60 000 years old (and could be less than 10 000 years old);
2) the level of carbon-14 has been varying during all the past (and present) and so we cannot know the level when our tree was chopped down. So, we cannot know its age.

Rock dating

There are different ways of using the different radioactive clocks for the inanimate rocks, but they can (for simplicity) be treated as a whole since they have common problems. We can measure how much of the material is left and we devise methods which, in principle, give us a reasonable estimate of what we started with. For example, if an isotope A is converted to isotope B, we can measure both and estimate how long the process has taken (figure 22).

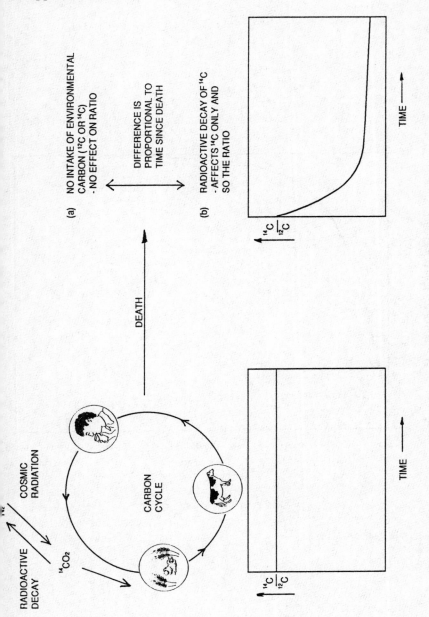

Figure 20: The carbon cycle and carbon-14 dating.

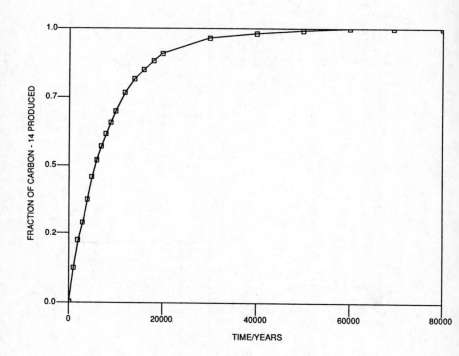

Figure 21: Growth curve for carbon-14.

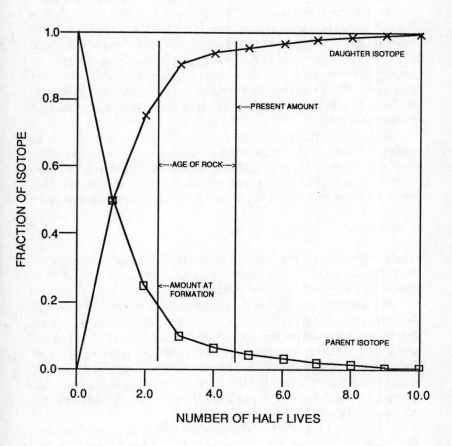

Figure 22: Rock-dating from growth and decay curves.

But, the problems are similar to those in our candle analogy. Can we be sure that we have not lost any A or B? Can we be sure that there was no B there at the beginning? The answer is always, no. If B is a gas, it may escape from the rock. If the rock was under water at anytime, the water may have washed out either of these elements.

We know that, in cases where the rocks have formed in historical times, they give dates implying hundreds of millions of years old. Rocks formed in Hualalei in 1801 give ages from 160 million to 3 000 million years! Different dating methods often give incompatible dates.

But, did you realise that most rocks cannot be dated radiometrically? The impression is given that all rocks can have their age measured. As any geologist will tell you, we cannot date sedimentary rocks — only volcanic and similar materials. That excludes most rocks and, in particular, those containing fossils!!

Conclusion

There is no independent test to help us check the ages estimated by radiometric means. The ages calculated are accepted if they conform to the evolutionary model.

We find coal deposits in the *carboniferous* period. This period occurred, according to evolutionists, around 300 million years ago. So, the coal should be that old. Since the carbon-14 should fade away by 100 000 years, the coal should not have a carbon-14 age: the radiation would have disappeared millions of years ago. BUT, even without correcting for the problem mentioned above, coal gives a carbon-14 age of about 30 000 years. So, the surrounding rocks must have a similar age.

The rock ages quoted in literature are fiction and based on false premises. The data measured can equally well be explained by the chemicals mixing during formation and crystallization.

Appendix C
A short bibliography

(a) *The Biblical Basis*

N Cameron	'Evolution and the Authority of the Bible' (Paternoster Press)
W W Fields	'Unformed & Unfilled' (Presbyterian & Reformed)
F Schaeffer	'Genesis in Space & Time' (Crossway Books)
E J Young	'Studies in Genesis 1' (Presbyterian & Reformed)
E J Young	'Genesis 3' (Banner of Truth Trust)
E J Young	'In the Beginning' (Banner of Truth Trust)

(b) *Popular scientific approaches*

E H Andrews	'From Nothing to Nature' (Evangelical Press)
S Tyler & A Gough	'Evolution: Is it Scientific'? (Christian Publicity Organisation)
A J Monty White	'Wonderfully Made' (Evangelical Press)
M Bowden	'Science vs Evolution' (Sovereign Publications)

(c) *Scientific publications by evangelicals*
1. *General*

E H Andrews, W Gitt, W J Ouweneel

'Concepts in Creationism' (Evangelical Press)

P Davis & C B Thaxton
                      'Pandas and People' (Haughton
                      Publishing Company)
L P Lester & R G Bohlin
                      'The Natural Limits to Biological
                      Change' (Probe Books)
J Scheven   'Mega-Sukzessionen und Klimax im
                      Tertiar' (German!) (Wort und Wissen)
J Scheven   'Daten zur Evolutionslehre im Biologie-
                      unterricht' (German!) (Wort und
                      Wissen)
A E Wilder-Smith,   'The Natural Sciences Know Nothing of
                      Evolution' (Master Books)

2. *Fossils*
J K Anderson & G Coffin
                      'Fossils in Focus' (Zondervan)
D T Gish   'The Fossils say No!' (Creation-Life
                      Publishers)
M L Lubenow   'Bones of Contention' (Baker Book
                      House)

3. *Chemical evolution*
S E Aw   'Chemical Evolution' (Master Books)
L R Croft   'How Life Began' (Evangelical Press)
C B Thaxton, W L Bradley, R L Olsen
                      'The Mystery of Life's Origin'
                      (Philosophical Library)

(d) *Scientific publications (by non-christians)*
M Denton   'Evolution in a Crisis' (Burnett Books)
F Hoyle & N C Wickramasinghe
                      'Evolution from Space' (Dent)
P E Johnson   'Darwin on Trial' (Regnery Gateway)
R Milton   'The Facts of Life - Shattering the Myth
                      of Darwinism' (Fourth Estate)
(e) *Journal*
Recommended :   'Origins' published by Biblical Creation
                      Society.

Appendix D
Glossary of scientific and theological terms

Amino acids   Small naturally-occurring chemical units that join to form proteins

Babel   Building erected by early man to usurp God's sovereignty (Genesis 11)

Bacteriophage   A virus that attacks a bacterium

Catalyst   A substance that accelerates a chemical change

Cenozoic   Term used to describe the most recent rock strata which include human remains

Cranium   Part of the skull covering the brain

Creation   Name given to the miraculous process by which God brought the universe into being at his command

Cubit   A distance corresponding to the length of the forearm

Cytoplasm   The main part of the cell surrounding the nucleus

Dinosaurs	Name of a group of animals, generally large, meaning 'terrible lizards'
DNA	Short for *deoxyribonucleic acid*, the chemical holding the genetic information
Ecosystems	The biological community containing the living organisms and their environment
Enzymes	Catalysts produced by a living organism
Evolution	Name given to the process of biological change, frequently applied specifically to the process in which it is postulated that modern organisms developed gradually and randomly from an original primitive cell
Fall	Term applied to the historical incident in which man fell from his state of innocence by sinning against God (Genesis 3)
Federal head	The legal representative of the human race
Fossils	Remains of animals or plants, or their impressions, found in rocks
Gene	The section of DNA carrying a unit of hereditary information
Haemoglobin	A red pigment in the blood which carries oxygen in the red-blood cells
Inhibitor	A substance that prevents a chemical change occurring

Jurassic	Rocks originally identified in the Jura mountains
Masoretic text	The copies of the biblical documents written by the Jewish scholars, the Masoretes
Metabolism	The chemical processes occurring in a living cell
Miocene	One of the groups of rocks occurring in the Cenozoic era
Molecules	The smallest unit of a chemical
Mutation	The process of biological change in the genes resulting in a change in hereditable characteristics. (Contrast God, who is *immutable*, unchanging)
Non-oxidising	An environment which prevents interaction with oxygen
Oxidation	The process in which a substance interacts with oxygen, releasing energy
Palaeozoic	Oldest group of rocks containing fossil remains; means 'Ancient life'
Peleg	Means 'division'; name of man born when the earth was divided (Genesis 10:25)
Phylum	One of the categories used to classify animals
Precambrian	The group of rocks preceding the Palaeozoic era containing little trace of life

Protein	A group of chemicals which occur in muscles, skin, hair, enzymes, etc.
Pyroclastic	Rocks formed as a result of volcanic eruptions
Redemption	Deliverance from some evil (e.g. slavery) by payment of a price; applied to price paid by Christ to deliver us
Samaritan text	The copy of the Pentateuch (first five books of the Old Testament) compiled by the Samaritans.
Science	The realm of knowledge about nature and the investigation of the underlying processes, whether mechanistic or miraculous
Septuagint text	The Old Testament text translated from the Hebrew by a group of Greek scholars
Sickle cell anaemia	A deficiency in the blood preventing the efficient uptake of oxygen due, in this case, to a deformation of the cell resulting in a sickle shape
Sin	The action of man, and his natural state, which is in rebellion to God, characterised, for example, by the breaking of his laws
Symbiosis	Process in which two organisms live in dependence on each other
Synclines	A trough in a rock-bed
Ultraviolet	A form of high energy radiation invisible to the human eye and emitted by the sun

Vertebrates   A group of animals with a backbone

Vestigial organs   Name given to those organs which are
                         believed by evolutionists to be remnants
                         of previous animal forms which are no
                         longer of use and are redundant.

Virus   Microscopic organism that replicates
                         itself by infecting a living organism

Index